CLIP ART

FOR YEAR A

STEVE ERSPAMER, SM

LITURGY TRAINING PUBLICATIONS

Duplicating the Art in This Book

The art in this book may be duplicated freely *by the purchaser* for use in a parish, school, community or other institution. This art may not be used on any materials that are intended to be sold.

CLIP ART FOR YEAR A
Copyright © 1992, Archdiocese of Chicago. All rights reserved.

Liturgy Training Publications
1800 North Hermitage Avenue
Chicago IL 60622-1101

Order Phone: 1-800-933-1800
FAX: 1-800-933-7094
Editorial Offices: 1-312-486-8970

Editor: Peter Mazar
Designer: Kerry Perlmutter

Printed in the United States of America
ISBN 0-929650-59-X
$25.00

Table of Contents

iv Introduction

1 **Advent Bulletin Cover**

2 First Sunday of Advent
3 Second Sunday of Advent
4 Immaculate Conception, December 8
5 Third Sunday of Advent
6 Fourth Sunday of Advent

7 **Christmastime Bulletin Cover**

8 Christmas Day, December 25
9 Sunday in the Octave of Christmas
10 Octave of Christmas, January 1
11 Epiphany of the Lord
12 Baptism of the Lord

13 **Winter Ordinary Time Bulletin Cover**

14 Second Sunday in Ordinary Time
15 Third Sunday in Ordinary Time
16 Fourth Sunday in Ordinary Time
17 Presentation of the Lord, February 2
18 Fifth Sunday in Ordinary Time
19 Sixth Sunday in Ordinary Time
20 Seventh Sunday in Ordinary Time
21 Eighth Sunday in Ordinary Time

22 **Lent Bulletin Cover**

23 Ash Wednesday
24 First Sunday of Lent
25 Second Sunday of Lent
26 Third Sunday of Lent
27 Fourth Sunday of Lent
28 Fifth Sunday of Lent
29 Palm Sunday of the Passion of the Lord

30 **Triduum Bulletin Cover**

31 Holy Thursday Evening
32 Good Friday
33 Easter Vigil

34 **Eastertime Bulletin Cover**

35 Easter Sunday
36 Second Sunday of Easter
37 Third Sunday of Easter
38 Fourth Sunday of Easter
39 Fifth Sunday of Easter
40 Sixth Sunday of Easter
41 Ascension of the Lord

42 Seventh Sunday of Easter
43 Pentecost

44 **Summer Ordinary Time Bulletin Cover**

45 Trinity Sunday
46 Body and Blood of Christ
47 Ninth Sunday in Ordinary Time
48 Tenth Sunday in Ordinary Time
49 Eleventh Sunday in Ordinary Time
50 Twelfth Sunday in Ordinary Time
51 Birth of St. John the Baptist, June 24
52 Thirteenth Sunday in Ordinary Time
53 Ss. Peter and Paul, June 29
54 Fourteenth Sunday in Ordinary Time
55 Fifteenth Sunday in Ordinary Time
56 Sixteenth Sunday in Ordinary Time
57 Seventeenth Sunday in Ordinary Time
58 Eighteenth Sunday in Ordinary Time
59 Transfiguration of the Lord, August 6
60 Nineteenth Sunday in Ordinary Time
61 Assumption of Mary, August 15
62 Twentieth Sunday in Ordinary Time
63 Twenty-first Sunday in Ordinary Time
64 Twenty-second Sunday in Ordinary Time
65 Twenty-third Sunday in Ordinary Time
66 Twenty-fourth Sunday in Ordinary Time
67 Triumph of the Cross, September 14

68 **Autumn Ordinary Time Bulletin Cover**

69 Twenty-fifth Sunday in Ordinary Time
70 Twenty-sixth Sunday in Ordinary Time
71 Twenty-seventh Sunday in Ordinary Time
72 Twenty-eighth Sunday in Ordinary Time
73 Twenty-ninth Sunday in Ordinary Time
74 Thirtieth Sunday in Ordinary Time
75 Thirty-first Sunday in Ordinary Time
76 All Saints, November 1
77 All Souls, November 2
78 Thirty-second Sunday in Ordinary Time
79 Dedication of the Lateran Basilica, November 9
80 Thirty-third Sunday in Ordinary Time
81 Christ the King

82 Thanksgiving Day
83 National Days

84 Subject Index

Introduction

"One picture is worth a thousand words." If that's true, you have an encyclopedia in your hands. This book contains close to 500 illustrations useful for bulletins, worship folders, calendars and handouts of every kind.

Each season and Sunday of the liturgical year has its own page; so do any feast days that can eclipse a Sunday. These are arranged in calendar order.

About the Artist and the Art

Steve Erspamer is a Marianist brother who makes his home in St. Louis, Missouri. He works with a multiplicity of media—clay, stone, fresco, art glass, silkscreened fabrics, block prints and, as this book demonstrates, cut paper.

Steve studied at St. Mary University in San Antonio, Texas; the Art Institute of San Antonio; Creighton University in Omaha; and Boston University. He has traveled in Western Europe and in India as a student of sacred art.

The artist brings to this book a respect for traditional iconography. In the positioning of the figures of Jesus and the Samaritan woman, in the depicting of a parable, even in the drawing of an apple, there are customary styles in Christian tradition. These forms have evolved, in part, because of their beauty and elegance, and also, in part, as expressions of the gospel of Christ and as emblems of the reign of God.

Many of the images in this book have been drawn in the style of stone carvings in Romanesque churches that dot the great medieval pilgrimage route through France and Spain. This style, in turn, borrows from Byzantine iconography. As examples of this style, incidental characters often are pictured smaller than main characters, disciples show their allegiance to Jesus by bowing, sometimes a figure will bend and twist to fit a form. All of this gives to the style a peculiar earthiness and playfulness.

Decoration sometimes adds another layer of meaning— tame animals suggest a return to paradise; wild animals suggest the Spirit's gift of fortitude; roses are signs of the flowering of God's reign; pomegranates represent the fruitfulness of the kingdom of heaven.

Iconographers ("image-writers") are held to an exacting discipline. According to the scriptures, Wisdom and the Word are God's image, embodied in Christ. And it is God's image, God's icon, in which we have been created. The iconographer attempts to create images of God's image. This cannot be done without humility, awe, even terror. That is why, in the tradition, an iconographer prepares to work by praying, fasting and almsgiving, and, according to custom, does not wear leather shoes while working. The artist becomes Moses standing before the burning bush!

Throughout this book, on the pages facing the art, are various suggestions and clues for using and understanding these images. The Sunday's or feast's calendar date is included here. The scriptures and psalm of the Mass are listed. There are brief explanations of the feast day or season. Here you also will find hints, on occasion, for paper and ink colors and for items to include in the bulletin or worship program that week.

Illustrations of the Sunday Readings

The book of scriptures read at the eucharist—the lectionary—is organized according to a few principles:

The first readings most often are from the books of Jewish scriptures, what Christians call the Old Testament. But during the fifty days of Eastertime, the first readings are from the Acts of the Apostles.

Second readings are usually from one of Paul's letters. They are read in sequence week by week through Ordinary Time. In the winter of Year A, we hear First Corinthians; in summer, Romans; in autumn, Philippians and First Thessalonians. We sometimes hear from the letters of authors other than Paul: During Eastertime this year, the second readings are taken from the First Letter of Peter.

Sunday gospels in Year A are most often from Matthew. But in Lent and Eastertime, every year, the gospels are usually from John.

In this clip art book, all the first readings and gospel readings of Year A have been illustrated, following the Roman Catholic lectionary for Mass. If you need illustrations for the second readings, they're here, too, but they may take a bit of searching to find.

For the second readings, a single piece of art sometimes can be used several Sundays in a row. For example, on page 73 you will find a "generic" illustration for all the Sundays when Paul's First Letter to the Thessalonians is proclaimed. And there may be more than one from which to choose: For example, other illustrations based on this letter can be found on pages 75, 78 and

80. The Index beginning on page 84 can help you locate appropriate art for the second readings.

There's an advantage to using the same illustration in bulletins and worship programs over the course of several weeks. It can be a wordless reminder that we are reading sequentially through a book. That piece of information too often gets lost.

The illustrations of the scripture readings were done in the same size: three-inch squares. That means you can depend on allotting the same area for each.

The scripture citations for Roman Catholics for the Mass readings and psalm are included in this book. Several citations may change when the revised lectionary for Mass is published in the mid-1990s.

Bulletin Covers

In this clip art collection, there is a full-page illustration for each season of the year. Use these for covers. They can be enlarged as posters for children to color. Of course, any of the pieces of art in this book can be enlarged to use as a bulletin or program cover.

Bulletin covers might change weekly or seasonally or for special occasions. Plot out a calendar to warn you when to give the printer any changes; some printers need covers weeks ahead of the insides of bulletins.

Art for Home, School and Parish Life

Throughout the book are all sorts of supplemental designs and images. They have been arranged according to the calendar: For instance, Valentine and Mardi Gras designs come in the winter, harvest and Halloween designs come in the autumn.

Sometimes an image from the Sunday psalm or entrance antiphon or sometimes a seasonal saint is depicted. Also, the artist brought to this book images from daily life—fireworks, bread baking, mothers and fathers, summer watermelon and winter mittens. These, too, are part of the language of liturgy.

Take advantage of the Index on page 84. It will help you find appropriate subjects.

Also in this book are a few pieces specifically for parish bulletins. On pages 70 to 73 are "logos" for worship schedules, wedding banns, server and lector schedules, choir rehearsals, and announcements to ushers and eucharistic ministers, as well as for mentioning who in the parish is in the catechumenate, who has been baptized, and who has died.

Use the Index to find useful art for confirmation, first communion, pancake breakfasts, potluck suppers, back-to-school announcements, and other parish and school events. (The books of Clip Art for Years B and C round out this collection.)

Using Clip Art and Preparing Handouts

Communications have become more visual and less verbal. Perhaps as a result of television, people are accustomed to complex visuals. They know when something looks unprofessional. That means that all of us who prepare parish bulletins, worship programs and the like are expected to produce sophisticated publications. That's hard work. It's skilled work, too, and it requires a sense of playfulness and creativity to do it well.

Here are a few hints: You probably don't need to be reminded of this, but it always takes longer than a person may first think to prepare a handout or bulletin.

In general, try not to mix typefaces; different sizes or degrees of boldness of the same typeface can be used instead. In a worship program, you'll likely be using music from various sources that have all sorts of typefaces. Why muddle the look of the program even more by using different faces for the headlines or instructions? Be careful when mixing styles of art; it's hard to do this well, and you may be able to achieve a more professional look if you stick to one style.

Use blank "white space" liberally—not every available corner of a handout should be filled. As a rule, make sure that both the words and the art have adequate space around them to give a clean look to the handout.

Occasionally, however, art and words (or music) can just about touch as long as the combination is sufficiently separated from other parts. For example, snowflakes can be overprinted in a pale color on top of the music to a carol; a figure can be positioned to appear to be standing on words; regular features in the bulletin can have a small piece of art set into the first lines of copy.

Investigate using unusual ink colors and papers; printers are happy to help. Allot time to proofread your work and to give a second look at the appropriateness of the art. Typographical or grammatical errors or a confusing layout will make a handout far less inviting to read.

Hold yourself to high standards. Ask other people's opinions. Emphasize the liturgical calendar in the parish bulletin, even if at times that means being at odds with other calendars. That might mean that Mother's Day gets a bit less attention than the season of Eastertime, that Valentine's Day gets no notice in years it falls right at the beginning of Lent, that the bulletin during Advent is free from Christmas images, and that during Christmastime the bulletin keeps up the spirit even if the shops have called it quits.

Be consistent in your designs. For example, in the bulletin, keep regular items—such as the worship schedule and wedding banns—in a regular position, and use the same heading and/or art for these items each week. Or you might make it a habit to use the worship folder as a "road map" of the liturgy: Highlight the basic structural elements as simply as you can.

It may take a year or more, but consistency pays off. If bulletins and worship aids and other handouts are done well, and if you prepare layouts that people can depend on, people will be able to make the best use of your work because they have learned where to find what they're looking for.

However, unusual happenings may call for unusual layouts. The Triduum or a parish renewal program or the coming of a holy day might mean that you skip any features in the bulletin in order to focus on the event at hand.

Be conservative with words and liberal with art. For example, a worship folder cover need not state the obvious—"Christmas," "Lent," "St. Mary's Church 100th Anniversary." Art usually doesn't need words to accompany it: An image of a jack o'lantern gets across the idea that here is something to do with Halloween.

Enlarge and reduce this art as needed. Some photocopiers can do that inexpensively. The art in this book was fashioned from cut paper. This style lends itself to the production of crisp enlargements and reductions. There is a point of diminishing returns, however: Be careful that the art is not enlarged so much that it becomes grotesque or reduced so much that it becomes undecipherable.

Because copies of copies sometimes lose definition, you may find it helpful to determine how the art and other elements of a handout will look when printed. You can estimate that by photocopying your layout. That's a handy trick to tell at a glance whether you've positioned the various elements attractively.

When preparing worship folders, try to enlarge words and music where appropriate—this can invite participation. Don't be afraid to make items as big as possible, as long as the whole is in scale.

Be conscientious about putting copyright notices where they are needed—for instance, in the acknowledgments on the back page of the program or, if required by the copyright owner, right alongside the copyrighted materials.

Omit unnecessary information. For example, hymn arrangements are frequently under copyright, and, if you copy these, you must include the necessary acknowledgments. But often the words and tunes of hymns are in the public domain. Give the publisher a phone call if you're not sure. Why complicate a handout with fine print if you don't have to?

You are free to copy the art in this book without acknowledgments if you use the art for a parish, a school or other institution. However, you may not use this art without written permission from Liturgy Training Publications if you sell the reproduction.

If you use a great deal of the art in this book through the year, please, at times, acknowledge the artist, the name of the book and the publisher. Users of parish and school handouts may appreciate the information. You may also consider, on occasion, providing explanations of the art you reproduce. Like most good things, visual images can get taken for granted. Often it's helpful to call attention to art and, at times, to explain images that may be unfamiliar.

Trust art to do its job. The word "illustrate" means to "make bright." That is certainly one of the goals of this book. Handouts made bright with art may be more appealing and can make the work of producing the handouts more worthwhile.

Because so much of this book is drawn from Christian tradition, there is a level of trust you can place in the art: Liturgical images can educate as well as illustrate. They teach without words. They tell stories, evoke moods and remind us of things we almost forgot. The images of this book do even more: They lead us into the lectionary, into the scriptures and psalms and even the spirit of the liturgy. They can lead us into mystery.

Search the art and study it and puzzle over it. You will find a language here that can give expression to faith. You will find images of God's image.

Wisdom is a breath of the power of God,
and a pure emanation of the glory of the Almighty.
For she is a reflection of eternal light,
a spotless mirror of the working of God.
—*Wisdom of Solomon 7:25, 26*

Christ is the image of the invisible God,
the firstborn of all creation.
—*Colossians 1:15*

Father, all-powerful and ever-living God,
we do well always and everywhere to give you thanks
through Jesus Christ our Lord.

In the wonder of the incarnation
your eternal Word has brought to the eyes of faith
a new and radiant vision of your glory.

In the Word we see our God made visible
and so are caught up in love of the God we cannot see.
—*from the first preface of Christmas*

All artists who, prompted by their talents,
desire to serve God's glory in holy Church,
should ever bear in mind that they are engaged
in a kind of sacred imitation of God the Creator.
—*Constitution on the Sacred Liturgy, #127*

The liturgy must be human as well as divine.
It should have participation and it should have art.
—*Reynold Hillenbrand, 1962*

Advent Bulletin Cover

Advent lasts from the fourth Sunday before
Christmas until sundown on Christmas Eve.

November 29 to December 24, 1992
December 3 to December 24, 1995
November 29 to December 24, 1998

Advent is an intense and short period of preparation for
Christmas. It is the church's tradition to keep this time
simply and soberly in the spirit of the liturgy. Images
woven through Advent are the preaching of John and
the prophets, the expectancy of Mary and Joseph,
the coming of Christ in glory to judge the world at the
end of time. Here is a mixture of harshness and ten-
derness, great challenge and great consolation.

Parish staffs have a yearlong obligation to encourage
an appreciation for the church's calendar. Perhaps during Advent this need is most pressing. Keeping Christian time is a kind of rehearsal for all the other times
when the gospel demands that we act in ways that
are countercultural, that are in opposition to commer-
cialism and materialism. There is difficult, challenging
work here.

In bulletins and other handouts, use this art to acquaint the
parish with Advent images. Save Christmas motifs, such
as holly and bells, for Christmastime. Paper and ink colors can reflect the seasons. Perhaps you can use purples, grays, blues and silvers during Advent. Hold off on
reds, whites, golds and greens until Christmas.

On Sundays in Year A, we hear Isaiah's strong words
about beating swords into ploughshares, about the
wolf being the guest of the lamb, about the lame dancing and the mute singing. Because these scriptures
are proclaimed every year at weekday Mass, every year
of the three-year cycle seems to include similar images
and emphases at this season.

Among other things, Advent is the church's face-to-face
encounter with the many moods of winter and all that win-
ter represents; teachers can turn to the images of winter instead of Christmas for Advent decorations in the
classroom. In this book are several wintry scenes in
the Advent and in the winter Ordinary Time sections.

The full-page art here depicts *Hagia Sophia,* Lady Wisdom, an image of Emmanuel, God with us. Other
art for Advent can also be found among the November
Sundays and feast days, pages 75–82.

ADVENT

First Sunday of Advent

violet

November 29, 1992
December 3, 1995
November 29, 1998

Isaiah 2:1−5
  Psalm 122
Romans 13:11−14
Matthew 24:37−44

All three readings are illustrated.

Please look over all the images in this book for Advent when choosing art for a particular occasion. Other images for early Advent can be found on the pages for late fall, 75−82. Also see pages 14 (candles in window), 41 (Christ enthroned), 56 (judge), 65 (watchman, lamp), 66 (Lord of the living and the dead).

Some parishes hand out this week (or the previous week) a special flyer with the Christmas worship schedule, perhaps with Advent prayers and songs, with instructions on how to build and use an Advent wreath, as well as with a schedule of any activities planned for Advent and for the Twelve Days of Christmas. You might use this flyer to inform the parish about the spirit of these seasons.

The Solemnity of the Immaculate Conception falls this week or next week. See the art for this day on page 4. The holy day worship schedule can be prominent in the bulletin. Of course, holy days need more attention in the bulletin than simply publishing the schedule. Consider preparing a page or special insert devoted to nothing but the holy day—its history and significance, meal prayers and songs for the day, and perhaps a few ideas for celebrating it in the home.

Second Sunday of Advent

violet

December 6, 1992
December 10, 1995
December 6, 1998

Isaiah 11:1–10
   Psalm 72
Romans 15:4–9
Matthew 3:1–12

All three readings are illustrated.

Note the image of St. Nicholas, whose memorial is December 6, as well as some other images sometimes associated with the day.

It's not too early to publish the parish Christmas worship schedule and to get the word out about activities planned for Christmastime.

PREPARE THE WAY OF THE LORD

4

Immaculate Conception

white

Tuesday, December 8, 1992
Friday, December 8, 1995
Tuesday, December 8, 1998

Genesis 3:9–15, 20
  Psalm 98
Ephesians 1:3–6, 11–12
Luke 1:26–38

An illustration of the first reading is found on page 24. Other appropriate images are found on Assumption Day, page 61. The art here is also appropriate for the feast of Our Lady of Guadalupe, December 12 (see also page 5).

In the bottom right corner is the Marian image of the Star of the Sea, who guides us to safe harbor in heaven. The center image shows Mary expectant with child. Although it may not be all that apparent, the images of the Immaculate Conception and of Our Lady of Guadalupe are of a pregnant woman clothed with the sun, with the moon at her feet (the image is taken from Revelation 12).

Third Sunday of Advent

rose or violet

December 13, 1992
December 17, 1995
December 13, 1998

Isaiah 35:1–6, 10
Psalm 146
James 5:7–10
Matthew 11:2–11

All three readings are illustrated. The coming of winter is underscored in the image of the patient farmer.

The Third Sunday of Advent was once called Gaudete (rejoice) Sunday, from the first word of the entrance antiphon for the day: "Rejoice in the Lord always; again I say, rejoice! The Lord is near" (Philippians 4:4, 5). In some parishes rose-colored vestments are worn. If this is your parish's practice, perhaps the Advent wreath can include a rose candle among the purple ones and the bulletin or other handouts can make use of this color (which is not pink but a dusky rose meant to soften somewhat the deep purple of the season).

Note the images of Our Lady of Guadalupe (December 12) and St. Lucy (December 13).

Fourth Sunday of Advent

violet

December 20, 1992
December 24, 1995
December 20, 1998

Isaiah 7:10–14
Psalm 24
Romans 1:1–7
Matthew 1:18–24

All three readings are illustrated.

The final Sunday of Advent falls within the period of the O Antiphons, December 17 to 23. These are seven prayers for the coming of Christ. One is prayed each day; it is the antiphon to the Canticle of Mary at Evening Prayer and the gospel acclamation at Mass. The O Antiphons are familiar in a hymn version in the song "O come, O come, Emmanuel." The seven antiphons are illustrated in a border on this page.

The "infancy narratives" are chapters 1 and 2 of Matthew and 1 and 2 of Luke. The parts of these narratives leading up to the birth of Jesus are proclaimed at weekday Mass during this final week of Advent. A passage from these narratives also is proclaimed on the Fourth Sunday of Advent every year. In Year A, we hear from Matthew about the annunciation to Joseph. This gospel is illustrated here.

In a sense, the final week of Advent is a kind of extension of Christmas Eve. There is intense final preparation. It's often a time, the last minute perhaps, for decorating, baking, cleaning, shopping. That is something of the mood of the liturgy this week.

The hectic atmosphere also surrounds the people who are responsible for bulletins, worship folders and other handouts. No doubt printers' deadlines are earlier than usual during the last few weeks of the year. Don't let the pressure make you miss an opportunity to organize something special for Christmas Day. Some parishes prepare a handout to welcome the many people who come to worship on this day. The handout can include prayers for the house, songs, blessings and perhaps an overview of programs and policies to invite folks to become involved in parish life.

7

Christmastime Bulletin Cover

Christmastime lasts from sundown on Christmas Eve until the feast of the Baptism of the Lord.

December 25, 1992, to January 10, 1993
December 25, 1995, to January 8, 1996
December 25, 1998, to January 10, 1999

Christmastime begins on Christmas Day and lasts well into January. Although there are changing emphases as the various feasts of Christmastime come and go—the nativity, the holy family, the motherhood of Mary, the naming of Jesus, the Epiphany, the baptism of the Lord—all these days are colored with the signs of Christmas.

Bear in mind that the first couple of Sundays of the new year are also Christmas Sundays. Even the parish bulletin can be a way to keep the Christmas spirit alive.

Red, white, gold and green are, of course, customary colors at Christmas. Using these colors for papers and inks after Christmas Day can help stress that the season continues until the feast of the Baptism of the Lord.

When searching for appropriate art for a particular feast or Sunday, select from all these Christmastime pages.

CHRISTMASTIME

8

Christmas Day

white

Friday, December 25, 1992
Monday, December 25, 1995
Friday, December 25, 1998

Vigil

Isaiah 62:1—5
Psalm 89
Acts 13:16—17, 22—25
Matthew 1:1—25

Dawn

Isaiah 62:11—12
Psalm 97
Titus 3:4—7
Luke 2:15—20

Night

Isaiah 9:1—6
Psalm 96
Titus 2:11—14
Luke 2:1—14

Day

Isaiah 52:7—10
Psalm 98
Hebrews 1:1—6
John 1:1—18

Other art for Christmas Day can be found on pages 6, 9 and 10.

When using the bulletin to offer good wishes, perhaps it's better and more personal to do so as individuals (for instance, "Monica Frederick" and "Sister John Bernard") and not on behalf of others ("the parish staff") or on behalf of the entire parish.

Christmas Day requires our best efforts at hospitality. However, mentioning twice-a-year worshipers, even to welcome them, can make everyone uncomfortable.

Christmas Eve and Day are premier occasions for advertising parish programs and ministries—everything from how to enroll a child as an altar server to how to get involved in a meals-on-wheels program. Perhaps the most natural way to welcome people is to give them something to do, which is an act of trust and reliance.

9

Sunday in the Octave of Christmas

white

Feast of the Holy Family

December 27, 1992

December 31, 1995

December 27, 1998

Sirach 3:2–6, 12–14

   Psalm 128

Colossians 3:12–21

Matthew 2:13–15, 19–23

The parish bulletin can help keep the Christmas spirit (and good wishes) alive. Other art for this weekend can be found throughout this Christmastime section. Art for the New Year is on page 10.

Octave of Christmas

white

Mary, Mother of God
The Name of Jesus

Friday, January 1, 1993
Monday, January 1, 1996
Friday, January 1, 1999

Numbers 6:22–27
   Psalm 67
Galatians 4:4–7
Luke 2:16–21

Liturgically speaking, January 1 is a complicated day.
First and foremost, it is the Octave of Christmas, New
Year's Day. The coming of Christ ushers in not merely
a new span of time but the eternal reign of God, the
fullness of time. The turning of the civil year is a symbol
of our entrance into eternity.

The church has given January 1 other titles, all related to
the day's gospel, Luke 2:16–21. We hear that the shepherds take up the song of the angels in proclaiming
God's peace on earth. We hear that Mary ponders
all these things in her heart. We hear of the circumcision and the naming of Jesus on the eighth day after
his birth.

The unique Roman Catholic title for this day is "Mary,
Mother of God." The title in Latin is *Maria, Dei Genitrix,*
Mary, the Bearer of God, which translates the Greek
term *Theotokos.* This is perhaps the oldest title of Mary.
Today is a celebration of Mary in Christmastime. (For
other art, see pages 4 and 61.)

The day has also been named World Day of Prayer for
Peace. In the Byzantine calendar, January 1 is the Circumcision of the Lord (the old title in the Roman calendar). In the Lutheran and Episcopalian calendars,
the day is the feast of the Holy Name of Jesus.

The figure of "Father Time" is related in folklore to Pope
Sylvester I, whose memorial is December 31. New
Year's Eve revelers sometimes are called "Sylvesters."
He called all the days of the year *feriae,* feast days. In
Christ, all time is now caught up in an endless festival.

Epiphany of the Lord

white

for Roman Catholics in the U.S.A. and Canada:

Sunday, January 3, 1993

Sunday, January 7, 1996

Sunday, January 3, 1999

for other Christians:

Wednesday, January 6, 1993

Saturday, January 6, 1996

Wednesday, January 6, 1999

Isaiah 60:1–6

Psalm 72

Ephesians 3:2–3, 5–6

Matthew 2:1–12

Epiphany is one of the greatest days on the church's calendar. It is a day of superlatives. Whatever was silent, dark and home-centered about Christmas is now boisterous, brilliant and community-oriented. Epiphany means "revelation." The promise of Advent is brought to fulfillment. Epiphany is a triple celebration of the revealing of Christ to the Magi, to people gathered at the Jordan when Jesus was baptized by John and to the wedding guests at Cana.

Sometimes today is called "Three Kings Day." That title focuses on one aspect of the mystery of this day, but this aspect is wonderful and popular and richly imaginative. The mix of races and peoples and languages that have come to be associated with the Magi makes the day something like Pentecost—a time to celebrate all the peoples and cultures of the planet.

Unfortunately, Epiphany is easy to neglect. Most everyone is exhausted from Christmas. The holidays mean that printers' deadlines are no doubt pushed backward. The Epiphany bulletin and other handouts may need to be completed in the middle of the Christmas rush. Perhaps it would be best to have an "artificial deadline" for Epiphany materials sometime in November or early Advent to give them the attention they deserve.

You might call folks' attention to the Blessing of the Home on Epiphany in *Catholic Household Blessings and Prayers.* This is a good weekend to make this book available for purchase. The school days near Epiphany are perfect for Christmas pageants and school parties.

12

Baptism of the Lord

white

for Roman Catholics in the U.S.A. and Canada:

Sunday, January 10, 1993
Monday, January 8, 1996
Sunday, January 10, 1999

for some other Christian churches:

Sunday, January 10, 1993
Sunday, January 7, 1996
Sunday, January 10, 1999

Isaiah 42:1–4, 6–7
  Psalm 29
Acts 10:34–38
Matthew 3:13–17

St. Maximus of Turin, a fourth-century bishop, set the birth and the baptism of the Lord side by side as equal reasons for joy: "At Christmas, Christ's mother Mary held him close to her heart. Today, God the Father embraces Christ as the beloved."

This feast is a continuation of Epiphany and the conclusion to Christmastime. The parish bulletin should be clear that it's still the Christmas season. Other appropriate art for the feast can be found on page 14.

Week 1 of Ordinary Time begins the day after this feast.
The scripture readings at the eucharist for the Second Sunday in Ordinary Time (next Sunday) continue the imagery of the baptism of the Lord.

RIVER JORDAN

Winter Ordinary Time Bulletin Cover

Monday, January 11, to Shrove Tuesday, February 23, 1993
Tuesday, January 9, to Shrove Tuesday, February 20, 1996
Monday, January 11, to Shrove Tuesday, February 16, 1999

Ordinary Time is not a church season as such. The term is a bit of jargon to describe the weeks in between the seasons. The word "ordinary" here means "ordinal," counted. The weeks of this "counted time" are each given a number to help the church organize its liturgical books.

Although Ordinary Time doesn't have sacred significance the way the seasons of Advent, Christmastime, Lent, Triduum and Eastertime do, these "in-between weeks" take on some of the imagery of the seasons of nature, of the civil calendar, and certainly of the scriptures, prayers and songs of the liturgy.

The gospels at Sunday Mass during winter Ordinary Time in Year A are mostly from the beginning of Matthew. The second readings are all from 1 Corinthians (for a "generic" piece of art good for all these Sundays, see page 14).

In their own way, the scriptures and psalms of these weeks seem to reflect Epiphany, with frequent images of light and the coming of the kingdom of heaven (see pages 14, 16–18, 21). And they seem to prepare for Lent, with Jesus and John's calls for discipleship and repentance, and with the often demanding teachings of the Sermon on the Mount (for art, see pages 14–16, 18–21).

In the span of Ordinary Time between Christmas and Lent, these are winter weeks (for art, see pages 5, 10, 14, 18, 20). Perhaps that means ice, rain and snow in your region, perhaps it means an influx of tourists. St. Valentine's Day is probably the biggest celebration on social calendars (see page 19). The feast of the Presentation is the biggest on the church's calendar (see page 17).

Carnival—a word that means "putting aside meat" and "farewell to the flesh"—starts when Christmas ends and ends as Lent starts (for art, see page 19). Along the Gulf Coast, Carnival is big business. In other places, it's unknown. Carnival celebrations began as a Christian antidote to the isolation caused by winter and as a preparation for the demands of lenten fasting. Perhaps these things—an antidote to winter and a preparation for Lent—are still needed by our church.

WiNTER

14

Second Sunday in Ordinary Time

green

January 17, 1993
January 14, 1996
January 17, 1999

Isaiah 49:3, 5–6
  Psalm 40
1 Corinthians 1:1–3
John 1:29–34

All three readings are illustrated.

On the Second through Eighth Sundays in Ordinary Time of Year A, the second readings are from the First Letter of Paul to the Corinthians. The art in the lower left-hand corner of this page can be used to illustrate the letter on any occasion that it is proclaimed at worship.

Note the wintertime images that may be useful from now through Lent (depending on how winter looks in your own neck of the woods). The gospel for this Second Sunday in Ordinary Time is John's account of the baptism of the Lord. Some of the art on page 12 is also appropriate for this Sunday.

Art for the Martin Luther King, Jr., holiday is on page 83.

CORINTH

15

Third Sunday in Ordinary Time

green

January 24, 1993
January 21, 1996
January 24, 1999

Isaiah 8:23 — 9:3
  Psalm 27
1 Corinthians 1:10 – 13, 17
Matthew 4:12 – 23

For an illustration for the second reading, see page 14.

This is the first of several weeks that Matthew is proclaimed at Sunday worship. Matthew's gospel will be read throughout Ordinary Time in Year A. You may want to highlight that today. The call of Matthew is the gospel for the Tenth Sunday in Ordinary Time; see page 48.

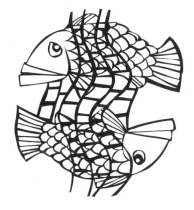

16

Fourth Sunday in Ordinary Time

green

January 31, 1993
January 28, 1996
January 31, 1999

Zephaniah 2:3; 3:12–13
   Psalm 146
1 Corinthians 1:26–31
Matthew 5:1–12

For an illustration for the second reading, see page 14.

In Year A, the Sermon on the Mount is proclaimed at Sunday worship from now until Ash Wednesday. At the bottom center of the next page is art depicting Christ the teacher. The center image on the page may be appropriate for Catholic Schools Week.

17

Presentation of the Lord

white

Tuesday, February 2, 1993
Friday, February 2, 1996
Tuesday, February 2, 1999

Malachi 3:1–4
  Psalm 24
Hebrews 2:14–18
Luke 2:22–40

This day is also called Candlemas. Candles are blessed this day to acclaim Christ the light of the world. February 2 is 40 days after Christmas. On Candlemas we take a last look back at Christmas and we take our first look forward to Easter. Lent is only a few weeks away.

In many places, it is customary to leave the nativity scene up until today. Other appropriate images for this feast are candles, doves, spring flowers and snowflakes. Just as old age took infancy into its arms in the meeting of Simeon, Anna and Jesus, winter and springtime seem to "meet" on this great feast day.

ANNA

18

Fifth Sunday in Ordinary Time

green

February 7, 1993
February 4, 1996
February 7, 1999

Isaiah 58:7–10
   Psalm 112
1 Corinthians 2:1–5
Matthew 5:13–16

For an illustration for the second reading, see page 14.

Notice how the first reading and the gospel focus on the imagery of light. We will hear a fuller version of the reading from Isaiah at the eucharist of the first Friday of Lent. All three of these Sunday readings fit well in preparing us for Lent. The parish bulletin, worship programs and other handouts can now be geared to preparation for the coming season. See the suggestions on page 23.

Art for Lincoln's Birthday, February 12, is on page 83.

19

Sixth Sunday in Ordinary Time

green

February 14, 1993
February 11, 1996
February 14, 1999

Sirach 15:15–20
Psalm 119
1 Corinthians 2:6–10
Matthew 5:17–37

For an illustration for the second reading, see page 14.

Efforts in the bulletin to prepare us for the coming season can be well underway. (See the notes on pages 22 and 23.) In 1999, this is the final Sunday before Ash Wednesday. The readings are superb in preparation for Lent.

Art for the national holidays in February is on page 83 Art for St. Valentine's Day and for Carnival (Mardi Gras) is found here.

20

Seventh Sunday in Ordinary Time

green

February 21, 1993
February 18, 1996

Leviticus 19:1–2, 17–18
  Psalm 103
1 Corinthians 3:16–23
Matthew 5:38–48

All three readings are illustrated. For an additional illustration for the second reading, see page 14.

In 1993 and 1996, this is the final Sunday before Ash Wednesday. The readings fit the spirit of preparation. Art for Carnival (Mardi Gras) is on page 19.

LOVE YOUR NEIGHBOR AS YOUR SELF

21

Eighth Sunday in Ordinary Time

green

Isaiah 49:14–15
  Psalm 62
1 Corinthians 4:1–5
Matthew 6:24–34

Two illustrations are provided for the gospel. For an illustration for the second reading, see page 14.

There is no Eighth Sunday in Ordinary Time in 1993, 1996 or 1999. (However, the scriptures for this Sunday are excellent for lenten preparation.) Some of the art here is also useful for Mother's Day.

22

Lent Bulletin Cover

Lent lasts from Ash Wednesday until Holy Thursday sundown.

Ash Wednesday, February 24, to Holy Thursday, April 8, 1993
Ash Wednesday, February 21, to Holy Thursday, April 4, 1996
Ash Wednesday, February 17, to Holy Thursday, April 1, 1999

Lent lasts from Ash Wednesday until Holy Thursday at sundown, when the Paschal Triduum begins. Lent is 40 days. The 40th day is Holy Thursday; the first day is the First Sunday. The four days from Ash Wednesday until that Sunday are a kind of lead-in to the season.

Another "40" is the 40 days of fasting: 38 days of the lenten fast (from Ash Wednesday until Holy Thursday, not counting Sundays) plus the 2 days of the paschal fast of Good Friday and Holy Saturday.

Colors associated with the season are purples, grays, browns, buffs and sometimes green.

The word Lent comes from "lengthen," because daytime grows longer during Lent. So Lent is an old word for the season of spring (for art, see pages 23, 24, 25). This is not necessarily the spring of flowers and bird songs; rather, it is the thawing of the land, the almost blinding light after the darkness of winter, the first small signs of life in an earth littered with death.

The lenten scriptures of Year A are associated with the final preparations for baptism at Easter. The readings for the third, fourth and fifth Sundays of Lent of Year A (pages 26–28) are used every year if the scrutiny rites are celebrated with the "elect," the catechumens chosen for baptism at Easter.

The coming of Easter and Eastertime itself brings out the best in the church's imagination. The richest and most varied scriptures, psalms, rites and sacramentals are part of the paschal season. The art in this book can help bring these to mind.

REMEMBER, PEOPLE, YOU ARE DUST

LENT

Ash Wednesday

violet

February 24, 1993
February 21, 1996
February 17, 1999

Joel 2:12–18
   Psalm 51
2 Corinthians 5:20—6:2
Matthew 6:1–6, 16–18

You might prepare a schedule of lenten worship and other seasonal activities to send home today or the previous Sunday. Information about parish missions, small group meetings and lenten programs will require at least three or four weeks lead time to organize effectively.

Some parishes prepare a lenten booklet that has the hows and whys of prayer, fasting and almsgiving. It may include the names and addresses of local and global organizations that need donations of time, resources and money. It may also include a reading list and even a video list (and local sources). An explanation of fasting (something more than regulations, something that speaks of the spirit and the broad possibilities of this practice) is needed. A first-person "pep talk" here can help to encourage a vigorous keeping of the season and an opening up of the religious imagination.

You can include in this handout the schedule for the liturgies of the Paschal Triduum. Make the distinction between Lent (which ends on Holy Thursday at sundown) and the Triduum (which then begins). Also make a distinction between the lenten fast, done in dependence on God and in sorrow for sin, and the paschal fast of Good Friday and Holy Saturday, done in anticipation of the paschal feast.

Try to make it clear that Lent is a preparation for the Triduum, not just for Easter Sunday. The three days of the Paschal Triduum are not a preparation for Easter. They *are* Easter!

Fish are associated with Christ and with lenten fasting. Images of fish can be found on pages 12, 15 and 58. Skulls are emblems of sin and death; these are on pages 28 and 75. Various images of the cross can be found on page 67.

24

First Sunday of Lent

violet

February 28, 1993
February 25, 1996
February 21, 1999

Genesis 2:7–9; 3:1–7
  Psalm 51
Romans 5:12–19
Matthew 4:1–11

Two illustrations of the gospel are provided. For the second reading, the image in the upper right corner is appropriate, or the illustration of Christ, the "new Adam" (on page 50) can be used.

The piggy bank represents almsgiving. The bank sits on the table all Lent as a promise of the coming Easter feast. Money is added each day. The bank is cracked open on Holy Thursday, and the money is brought to church for the special collection for the poor.

How else will parishioners be collecting alms? To whom are the money and resources pledged? The bulletin can be used to make people aware of the recipients of lenten alms. Also, local organizations that may need more muscle than money can be listed and explained.

Second Sunday of Lent

violet

March 7, 1993
March 3, 1996
February 28, 1999

Genesis 12:1–4
   Psalm 33
2 Timothy 1:8–10
Matthew 17:1–9

Two illustrations of the gospel are provided. Another image of the Transfiguration is found on page 59. For the second reading, use one of the illustrations of the Transfiguration or use the servant image in the center left of page 21.

The scorpion and snake, desert creatures, represent the "sting" of death and sin (1 Corinthians 15:56). These are strong and ancient emblems of Lent.

MOSES   ELIJAH

26

Third Sunday of Lent

violet

March 14, 1993
March 10, 1996
March 7, 1999

Exodus 17:3–7
   Psalm 95
Romans 5:1–2, 5–8
John 4:5–42

All three readings are illustrated.

The burning bush and the water from the rock are powerful lenten symbols. They are emblems for the Sunday eucharist, our encounter with God, our oasis in the journey. The soup pot can represent the simple living of this season of fasting. This art can be used for parish suppers during Lent.

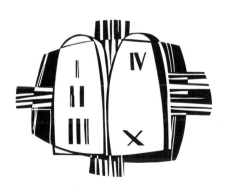

27

Fourth Sunday of Lent

rose or violet

March 21, 1993
March 17, 1996
March 14, 1999

1 Samuel 16:1, 6–7, 10–13
   Psalm 23
Ephesians 5:8–14
John 9:1–41

All three readings are illustrated.

The Fourth Sunday in Lent was previously called Laetare (rejoice) Sunday, from the first word of the entrance antiphon for the day, "Rejoice, Jerusalem! Be glad for her, you who love her. . . ." At this midpoint in Lent, we catch our first sight of Jerusalem, our destination, our homeland, the place of death, burial and resurrection. See art on pages 11, 39 and 79. The opening prayer for this Sunday includes the line "Let us hasten to Easter." Our lenten journey is now a race.

There is another reason for rejoicing. This day often falls near the spring equinox. The rose-colored vestments used in some parishes on this day soften the lenten purple and call to mind the flowering of spring. Other images of roses and spring flowers are on pages 6, 9, 20, 24 and 25.

At this time of year come St. Patrick's Day, March 17, the solemnity of St. Joseph, March 19, and the solemnity of the Annunciation, March 25. On page 28 are shamrocks. Art for St. Joseph's Day and Annunciation Day is on pages 4, 6, 8 and 9. Give Lent a little more prominence in the bulletin than these feast days.

Live as children of the light * Live as children of the light * Live as children of the light * Live as children of the light

LAETARE

REJOICE

28

Fifth Sunday of Lent

violet

March 28, 1993
March 24, 1996
March 21, 1999

Ezekiel 37:12–14
  Psalm 130
Romans 8:8–11
John 11:1–45

For an illustration of the second reading, use the "generic" illustration of Paul's Letter to the Romans (on page 62), or use the center left-hand illustration found on page 43.

Although shamrocks are associated with St. Patrick's Day, March 17, they are fitting emblems throughout Lent. Patrick held up the shamrock to teach catechumens about the Holy Trinity. People reconciling with the church at Easter were once decked with spring greenery as a sign of forgiveness and regeneration.

Incense is used year-round at worship, but it is particularly associated with Lent. Incense is a tree resin that melts and vaporizes when heated, a sign of self-sacrifice and prayer. The smoke was thought to purify whatever it surrounded. Because incense drips from the wounded bark of certain trees, folktales about incense call it the "tears" of weeping trees, and so incense became a sign of sorrow.

During the singing of Psalm 141 at Evening Prayer, incense is offered by the church in sorrow for the sins of the world. Other art depicting incense is on pages 9, 65 and 71.

Palm Sunday of the Passion of the Lord

red

April 4, 1993
March 31, 1996
March 28, 1999

Matthew 21:1–11
Isaiah 50:4–7
   Psalm 22
Philippians 2:6–11
Matthew 26:14—27:66

The liturgy (and even the title) for this Sunday has a split personality. First, it is Palm Sunday, the day we welcome the Messiah into the holy city of Jerusalem to begin the Passover. Second, it is Passion Sunday, the day we proclaim the gospel of Jesus' suffering and death.

The liturgy includes both the triumphal entrance and the passion, but these two are not "blended." On a several-page program, only the pages that cover the entrance liturgy would depict the entrance; remaining pages would use art depicting the passion.

The color for this day is red. Royal scarlets and purples, as well as the greens and browns of the branches, are colors associated with this Sunday. Images for the triumphal entrance are palms, pussy willows, olives, Jerusalem, the paschal lamb, the assembly of the saints; see pages 11, 23, 36–39, 46, 53, 76 and 79. Images of the cross and passion are on pages 32, 49 and 67. The second reading (from Philippians) is illustrated on the top center of page 70.

This last Sunday of Lent has a practical function. The liturgy just about shouts that the Passover is almost here. From now until Holy Thursday evening we have a few final days to get ready. If we ignored Lent up until now, here is our Lent. If we kept Lent wholeheartedly, then we enter more deeply into preparations.

Some parishes put together a special worship folder or bulletin insert to be taken home this weekend. It includes a schedule of the Triduum liturgies and other events, such as the preparatory rites with the elect, parish meals and the blessing of Easter foods. Also included are a "pep talk" about attending the liturgies, words of encouragement for keeping the paschal fast on Good Friday and Holy Saturday, and some encouragement to keep the days free from work, entertainment and shopping. (LTP publishes a bulletin insert for the Triduum, *Three Days to Save,* that includes a blank space on which to photocopy the parish schedule.)

30

Triduum Bulletin Cover

The Paschal Triduum of the death, burial and resurrection of the Lord lasts from Holy Thursday sundown until Easter Sunday sundown.

Holy Thursday, April 8, to Easter Sunday, April 11, 1993
Holy Thursday, April 4, to Easter Sunday, April 7, 1996
Holy Thursday, April 1, to Easter Sunday, April 4, 1999

Education about the Triduum and the building of enthusiasm and even a kind of deep piety for the Pasch belong often in the lenten homilies, bulletins, parish mission—and also in the religious education programs and the parish school. Here, too, art has an important place.

During these days, people are in church not out of habit but out of desire. There is a natural eagerness to be there. But the odd times of the services and the once-a-year rites can have the effect of turning even the most enthusiastic assembly into spectators. How can this be avoided?

You might remove from church the hymnals or other song booklets that are not needed. (This is hard work.) Ministers of hospitality can greet people with the participation aid. Design materials that need little explanation (also hard work, but good work, because frequent announcements of "Please turn to page such-and-such" seem out of character with the spirit of these days). If music is selected from the parish's year-round repertory, participation is enhanced. There will be a few once-a-year pieces, but if this music returns faithfully every year, it too becomes part of the repertory.

Participation aids for the Triduum can be streamlined; the print and music should be large; art may be used generously and can serve as visual clues to where we are in the liturgy. 8½" × 14" paper, folded in half, makes an attractive 8½" × 7" format. Or 8½" × 11" sheets can be collated and stapled along the 8½-inch edge for a "horizontal" (and handsome) booklet. If feasible, prepare the booklet so that art goes toward the inside, near the staples, and music goes toward the outside.

Extra effort (and extra expense) to have quality paper, stapling, and two- or three-color printing helps communicate the importance of these days (and can make the programs more inviting to pick up and use).

PASCHAL TRIDUM

31

Holy Thursday Evening

white

April 8, 1993
April 4, 1996
April 1, 1999

Exodus 12:1–8, 11–14
Psalm 116
I Corinthians 11:23–26
John 13:1–15

All three readings are illustrated. Other images appropriate to this night are on pages 29, 36–38, 46 and 75.

On Sundays, most people come and go with greetings, conversation and catching up on the events of the week. The Triduum has a different spirit. The Holy Thursday liturgy does not have a conclusion—there is no dismissal. The Good Friday liturgy has no greeting and no dismissal. Once the church gathers on Holy Thursday night, we see the Christian Passover through to its conclusion. There is the sense that the Triduum liturgies are really a single three-day-long service. So the comings and goings of the assembly are done privately, quietly.

Perhaps any worship aid for this evening can end with a well-worded invitation for people to remain in prayer. Also, you can politely request that when people come and go they do so in silence for the sake of those keeping watch. Each day's worship aid can include mention of the next important moment in the Triduum.

One parish puts together attractive signs for all the doorways. The signs are decorated with pussy willows and red ribbons. They read:

> **The church will remain open**
> **throughout these three holy days of Easter.**
> **Please come and go in silence**
> **for the sake of those at prayer.**

In the vestibule near the doorways are schedules of the Triduum liturgies. One parish has an artist prepare a large outdoor sign, which is readable to people who drive by, with the worship schedule and a few words of welcome: "Come to the Passover!"

32

Good Friday

red

April 9, 1993
April 5, 1996
April 2, 1999

Isaiah 52:13—53:12
  Psalm 31
Hebrews 4:14–16, 5:7–9
John 18:1—19:42

Other images of the cross and passion of Christ are on pages 29, 49 and 67.

The Good Friday bulletin or program can be used to remind the parish of the time of the Easter Vigil and of the preparatory rites with the elect, and to remind households to bring Easter food for the blessing. Consider adding an explanation of the paschal fast along with prayers and songs to use at home tonight and on Holy Saturday.

33

Easter Vigil

white

April 10, 1993
April 6, 1996
April 3, 1999

Genesis 1:1—2:2
   Psalm 104 (or Psalm 33)
Genesis 7:1–23; 8:1–19;
   9:8–15
   Psalm 46
Genesis 22:1–18
   Psalm 16
Exodus 14:15—15:1
   Exodus 15
Isaiah 54:5–14
   Psalm 30

Isaiah 55:1–11
   Isaiah 12 (or Psalm 51)
Baruch 3:9–15, 32—4:4
   Psalm 19:8–11
Ezekiel 36:16–28
   Psalms 42 and 43
Romans 6:3–11
   Psalm 118
Matthew 28:1–10

The preparation of a worship aid for the Easter Vigil liturgy is affected by a number of considerations: How much will be done in the darkness? Will the assembly move from place to place? How much of the singing can be done from memory rather than from the printed page? The music selected for this night can be responsorial style and acclamatory, rather than hymns, so the assembly does not have to rely heavily on a worship aid or hymnal. That can free people's hands and better enable the parish to celebrate the Vigil by candlelight.

Three of the Vigil readings are illustrated here: creation, the exodus and the angel at the tomb. Noah's dove is on page 12. The promise to Abraham is illustrated on page 48. Miriam dancing with her tambourine is depicted on page 54. An illustration appropriate for Isaiah 54:5–14 is in the upper center of page 80. An illustration of Isaiah 55:1–3 is in the upper right of page 58. An illustration of Isaiah 55:10 is in the upper center of page 55.

Illustrations appropriate for the Baruch reading are in the upper center of page 16 and the upper center of page 69. An illustration for Ezekiel 36:16–28 is in the upper right of page 28.

For the Romans reading, see page 62. The long border on the left side of page 52 illustrates Romans 6:3. Other art appropriate to christening is on pages 27 and 45 and throughout the Eastertime section.

34

Eastertime Bulletin Cover

Eastertime lasts from Easter Sunday until Pentecost.

Easter Sunday, April 11, to Pentecost, May 30, 1993
Easter Sunday, April 7, to Pentecost, May 26, 1996
Easter Sunday, April 4, to Pentecost, May 23, 1999

Eastertime is the church's most ancient season. It is the "week of weeks," 50 days, from Easter Sunday until Pentecost. During the 40 days of Lent the liturgy drew us into the mystery of exile. Now we are called to enter the mystery of homecoming. Eastertime can be more difficult to keep than Lent. We are challenged to live in peace, in righteousness, with our heads in heaven and with our hands at work.

The visuals and decorations used in church, in parish school classrooms, in the bulletin and worship programs can remind everyone that Easter lasts seven weeks.

Eastertime is a season of Christ's death, burial and resurrection, and of our baptism into that passover. There are a few signs of this passover that are familiar and strong—and perhaps overused—such as eggs and flowers and butterflies. And there are signs of Easter that are so common at this time of year that they may not be recognized as signs—first communions, a spring hailstorm, washing the car, Mother's Day, the school prom, tidying a grave, planting geraniums.

This book includes imagery of Eastertime from the tradition—the pelican, the paschal lamb, the gardener. You'll note on occasion a few words of explanation. It may be a service to parishioners to share some of these explanations of Christian symbolism.

EASTERTIME

35

Easter Sunday

white

April 11, 1993
April 7, 1996
April 4, 1999

Acts 10:34, 37–43
  Psalm 118
Colossians 3:1–4
  or 1 Corinthians 5:6–8
John 20:1–9
  or Matthew 28:1–10
  or Luke 24:13–35

Take advantage of the fine turnout on this day of days. Worship programs might be prepared with some basic catechesis about the Mass. Invite the assembly to take these programs home.

What would such education about the Mass be like? It would be subtle and carefully worded. Instructions on when to sit and stand may be good, but perhaps it would be better to explain briefly the reason why. For example, "We stand to listen to the gospel" may be better than "Stand for the gospel." See the order of Mass (pages 1–37) in *The Saint Andrew Bible Missal* (New York: William J. Hirten Co., Inc., 1982) for examples of brief explanations that might be used.

Including the titles of the parts of the liturgy may also be good, but that has to be done simply and with the correct typefaces. For instance, "liturgy of the word," "liturgy of baptism" and "liturgy of the eucharist" would all appear in the largest typeface.

You might prepare a parish handout or bulletin insert with meal prayers, songs, a home blessing and perhaps even Eastertime recipes and customs. Send these home along with a small container of Easter water. This is a fine day to make available for purchase *Catholic Household Blessings and Prayers*. Call folks' attention to the Eastertime blessings in this book.

Easter Sunday is a premier occasion for advertising parish programs and ministries—everything from how to join the choir to how to get involved in the seniors' program. Perhaps the most natural, most trusting way of welcoming people is to give them something to do. This may be more hospitable than calling everyone's attention to the swelled attendance this day.

36

Second Sunday of Easter

white

April 18, 1993
April 14, 1996
April 11, 1999

Acts 2:42–47
*   Psalm 118*
1 Peter 1:3–9
John 20:19–31

On Eastertime Sundays in Year A, the second readings at Mass are from the First Letter of Peter. For "generic" art for the second readings during this season, you can use the images in the top right corner of page 38.

The Easter season continues until Pentecost. School and parish bulletins and handouts can continue to look like Easter throughout these seven weeks of celebration.

This page and the next two pages include images of the paschal lamb. The lamb is the innocent sacrificial animal. The blood of newborn sheep and goats was sprinkled over doorways to mark the homes of the Hebrew slaves on the night of Passover, when the angel of death struck down all the firstborn of animals and people. The blood was a sign for the angel to spare the household.

We sing in the *Exsultet* of Easter Eve that "This is our passover feast, when Christ, the true Lamb, is slain, whose blood consecrates the homes of all believers." The baptized, "clothed in fine linen, bright and pure," are the bride of the Lamb of God. Easter is a taste of the marriage supper (Revelation 19:7–8).

Easter eggs and the Easter bunny are not "pagan" symbols, as sometimes is written. Eggs are likened to the tomb of Christ. They crack open to bring forth new life. Rabbits are associated with the dawn; they were thought to spend the night keeping watch for the first light of morning. (If you've ever caught rabbits munching merrily on your garden in the wee hours, you can understand why people thought this.) Strange as it sounds, Christians on Easter Eve are likened to rabbits; we kept vigil throughout the night in anticipation of the resurrection of all creation.

PEACE TO YOU

37

Third Sunday of Easter

white

April 25, 1993
April 21, 1996
April 18, 1999

Acts 2:14, 22–28
Psalm 16
I Peter 1:17–21
Luke 24:13–35

Animals that undergo a metamorphosis, such as butterflies, are Easter symbols of great antiquity. Images of
these animals can be found carved into ancient tombs.
On one sarcophagus, a frog (see page 36) is shown
emerging from a pond; nearby are carved the words
"in the twinkling of an eye." This is a reference to
I Corinthians 15:52. "We will all be changed, in a
moment, in the twinkling of an eye, at the last
trumpet." Metamorphosis is a Greek word meaning
a transfiguration, a transformed body.

38

Fourth Sunday of Easter

white

May 2, 1993
April 28, 1996
April 25, 1999

Acts 2:14, 36–41
  Psalm 23
1 Peter 2:20–25
John 10:1–10

All three readings are illustrated.

Today is sometimes called Good Shepherd Sunday because the gospels for the Fourth Sunday of Easter, always from John, deal with passages about shepherds and sheep. In the gospel of Year A, Jesus calls himself not the shepherd but the sheep gate that opens to safe, green pasture. However, the second reading (from 1 Peter), Psalm 23 and the gospel acclamation bring into the liturgy the powerful and familiar image of the Good Shepherd.

39

Fifth Sunday of Easter

white

May 9, 1993
May 5, 1996
May 2, 1999

Acts 6:1−7
  Psalm 33
1 Peter 2:4−9
John 14:1−12

All three readings are illustrated.

The Ascension holy day worship schedule (and schedule of other activities planned for this day) can be prominent in the bulletin this week and the next.

This page and the next have animal motifs associated with Eastertime. They are useful throughout the season.

The peacock is a symbol of the resurrection. Its spectacular plumage molts and then fresh feathers emerge. In ancient times, the peacock was identified with the phoenix bird, which, according to legend, made a nest in a date palm tree (itself a sign of resurrection) and then burst into flames. A red egg in the ashes hatched into a new and more splendid phoenix.

Again, according to legend, the pelican feeds its young on its own blood, and so the bird became an emblem of self-sacrifice. The peacock, pelican and phoenix are favorite Christian symbols that have been carved in the stonework of many churches.

The deer drinking from the fountain represents Psalm 42:1, "As a deer longs for flowing streams, so my soul longs for you, O God."

NICA NOR PHI LIP PRO CHO RUS STE PHEN PARM ENAS NICO LAUS TI M ON

40

Sixth Sunday of Easter

white

May 16, 1993
May 12, 1996
May 9, 1999

Acts 8:5–8, 14–17
Psalm 66
1 Peter 3:15–18
John 14:15–21

For an illustration of the second reading, you can use the crucifixion scene in the bottom center of page 32.

The Ascension holy day worship schedule (and schedule of other activities planned for this day) can be prominent in the bulletin this weekend.

50 DAYS FOR OUR DELIGHT: FOR CHRIST IS RISEN AS ALL THINGS TELL. GOOD CHRISTIANS, SEE YE RISE AS WELL .

PHILIP

41

Ascension of the Lord

white

In the U.S.A.:

Thursday, May 20, 1993
Thursday, May 16, 1996
Thursday, May 13, 1999

For Roman Catholics in Canada:

Sunday, May 23, 1993
Sunday, May 19, 1996
Sunday, May 16, 1999

Acts 1:1–11
    Psalm 47
Ephesians 1:17–23
Matthew 28:16–20

Easter is 50 days. On the 40th day we focus on the account, found in the beginning of the Acts of the Apostles, of Jesus' ascension into glory. According to the second reading for this solemnity, from Ephesians 1, "God has made Christ the head over all things for the church, which is the body of Christ, the fullness of Christ who fills all in all."

This day is not about departure or disappearance. It is about presence. "Not only are we confirmed today in our possession of paradise, but in Christ, who is the head of our body, we have begun the triumphal entry into the heaven of heavens." (Pope St. Leo of Rome, 5th century)

Eastertime continues with full vigor until Pentecost. The art in the bulletin and other parish publications can reflect this continuation.

42

Seventh Sunday of Easter

white

In Canada, this Sunday is observed as the Solemnity of the Ascension of the Lord.

May 23, 1993
May 19, 1996
May 16, 1999

Acts 1:12–14
   Psalm 27
1 Peter 4:13–16
John 17:1–11

The first reading is illustrated here. For illustrations of the other readings, the art on page 41 (of the ascension and glorification of Christ) can be used.

On Ascension Day we heard that two men in white garments told the onlookers, "This Jesus, who has been taken up from you into heaven, will come in the same way as you saw him go into heaven" (Acts 1:11).

In the next chapter of Acts, we hear that "suddenly from heaven there came a sound like the rush of a violent wind, and it filled the entire house where the disciples were sitting." According to the Book of Acts, Christ returns from heaven in the full and glorious power of the Spirit.

Ascension Day marks the beginning of the Pentecost novena, nine days of prayer for the coming of the Holy Spirit, who is the presence of God. The art on pages 41 to 43 is useful throughout the novena.

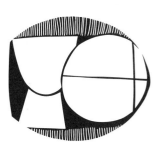

Pentecost

red

May 30, 1993
May 26, 1996
May 23, 1999

Vigil	**Day**
Genesis 11:1–9	*Acts 2:1–11*
or Exodus 19:3–8, 16–20	*Psalm 104*
or Ezekiel 37:1–14	*1 Corinthians 12:3–7, 12–13*
or Joel 3:1–5	*John 20:19–23*
Psalm 104	
Romans 8:22–27	
John 7:37–39	

The first two readings are illustrated here. For an illustration of the gospel, you can select one from page 36.

For the Vigil, the Exodus reading is illustrated in the upper right corner of page 47. Ezekiel is illustrated in the upper right corner of page 28. Romans is illustrated in the lower left of page 55. For other readings, the Pentecost illustrations here are appropriate. The art in the lower left of page 64 can be used to illustrate the gospel.

Pentecost is one of the greatest church festivals. Like Epiphany, it is a "conclusion" feast. The observance of Pentecost, like Epiphany, is communal, exuberant and public.

The spirit of a community-wide, outdoor celebration takes its cue from Acts 2:1–21. All nationalities gather in Jerusalem to keep the Jewish festival of *Shavuot* (meaning "Weeks" in Hebrew), and called, in Greek, Pentecost (meaning "50 days"—the feast falls seven weeks, 50 days, after Passover). Suddenly the disciples tumble into the streets under the prompting of the Spirit. The scene is so boisterous that the crowd thinks the disciples are drunk!

Shavuot **is also called, in Hebrew,** *Yom ha-Bikkurim,* **the Day of Firstfruits.** In Mediterranean lands (and in California and in the South), Pentecost is in fact the time of the first harvest—of grain, of strawberries, of cherries and apricots. (See the index to locate these images.) It has become customary to decorate synagogues and churches with fresh summer leaves and sheaves of grain. Using pentecostal imagery, St. Paul called Christ "the firstfruits of the dead" (1 Corinthians 15:20).

44

Summer Ordinary Time Bulletin Cover

Monday, May 31 to Monday, September 13, 1993
Monday, May 27 to Friday, September 13, 1996
Monday, May 24 to Monday, September 13, 1999

For an explanation of Ordinary Time, see page 13.

This book somewhat arbitrarily divides Ordinary Time into the three seasons of nature that Ordinary Time spans—winter, summer and fall. During the summer in Year A, the second reading is from Paul's Letter to the Romans. For a "generic" piece of art suitable for all these second readings from Romans, see page 62. Matthew is the gospel that we will be hearing through Ordinary Time this year. In this book, each Sunday's gospel passage is illustrated.

The summer period of Ordinary Time begins with two Sunday feasts—the Solemnity of the Most Holy Trinity and the Solemnity of the Body and Blood of Christ.

In 1993 and 1999, the Twentieth Sunday in Ordinary Time gets "eclipsed" by the Solemnity of the Assumption of Mary, August 15. Other than this, the sequence of Ordinary Time Sundays throughout summer and fall is not interrupted in 1993, 1996 or 1999.

The full-page art here depicts the parable of the sower and the seed (15th Sunday), the multiplication of the loaves and fishes (18th Sunday), and Jesus walking on water (19th Sunday).

Art for summertime national holidays is on pages 52, 54 and 83.

SUMMER

45

Trinity Sunday

white

June 6, 1993
June 2, 1996
May 30, 1999

Exodus 34:4–6, 8–9
  Daniel 3:52–56
2 Corinthians 13:11–13
John 3:16–18

An illustration of the first reading is in the upper right of page 47. An illustration appropriate for the second reading is in the lower right of page 40. To illustrate the gospel, an image of Christ would be appropriate; see, for example, the lower center of page 16.

Images of the Holy Trinity from the tradition are shamrocks (page 28); three intertwined fish; the human hand, a lamb and a dove; God's eye set within a triangle. The psalm for the Sunday Mass is the *Benedicite,* the song of the three children in the fiery furnace (Daniel 3).

46

Body and Blood of Christ

white

June 13, 1993
June 9, 1996
June 6, 1999

Deuteronomy 8:2–3, 14–16
Psalm 147
1 Corinthians 10:16–17
John 6:51–58

The art here is also useful for processions, first communions and for Holy Thursday.

An illustration of the first reading is in the upper right of page 47 (and the upper left of this page). An illustration appropriate for the second reading is in the bottom left of page 31. Any eucharistic image is appropriate to illustrate the gospel; see, for example, the upper right of page 36. Other appropriate art for this day can be found on pages 18, 29, 31, 37, 42, 49 and 69.

Ninth Sunday in Ordinary Time

green

Deuteronomy 11:18, 26—28
Psalm 31
Romans 3:21—25, 28
Matthew 7:21—27

For an illustration for the second reading, see page 62.

There is no Ninth Sunday in Ordinary Time in 1993, 1996 or 1999. However, some of the art here may be useful for the early summer.

Tenth Sunday in Ordinary Time

green

Hosea 6:3–6
Psalm 50
Romans 4:18–25
Matthew 9:9–13

All three readings are illustrated. For an additional illustration for the second reading, see page 62.

There is no Tenth Sunday in Ordinary Time in 1993, 1996 or 1999. Some of the subjects here (God's coming is as sure as the spring rain, God's promise to Abraham) are useful at other times of the year, especially at the Easter Vigil. The gospel this Sunday is Jesus' call of Matthew, the evangelist this year. You can use this image whenever you need to underscore the proclamation of the gospel according to Matthew.

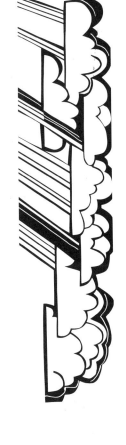

49

Eleventh Sunday in Ordinary Time

green

June 16, 1996
June 13, 1999

Exodus 19:2–6
  Psalm 100
Romans 5:6–11
Matthew 9:36—10:8

For an illustration for the second reading, see page 62.

Note the harvest images on this Sunday. Although city folk tend to associate the word "harvest" with autumn, in reality the "amber waves of grain" of the wheat harvest are ripe in early summer. Pentecost and Ss. Peter and Paul Day are, of old, wheat harvest celebrations. The grain harvest images from Matthew's gospel are well timed to this season of the year.

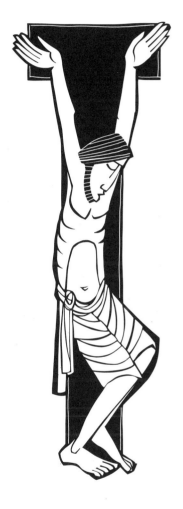

50

Twelfth Sunday in Ordinary Time

green

June 20, 1993
June 23, 1996
June 20, 1999

Jeremiah 20:10–13
   Psalm 69
Romans 5:12–15
Matthew 10:26–33

All three readings are illustrated.

On the Ninth through Twenty-fourth Sundays in Ordinary Time of Year A, the second readings are from the Letter of Paul to the Romans. The art in the upper right corner of this page is an illustration of Christ, the "new Adam," one of the strong themes of this letter of Paul. See also the "generic" art for this letter on page 62.

School's out! Images for summer camp, vacation Bible school or other summer programs are on pages 63 and 64.

51

Birth of St. John the Baptist

white

Thursday, June 24, 1993
Monday, June 24, 1996
Thursday, June 24, 1999

Vigil	**Day**
Jeremiah 1:4–10	*Isaiah 49:1–6*
Psalm 71	*Psalm 139*
1 Peter 1:8–12	*Acts 13:22–26*
Luke 1:5–17	*Luke 1:57–66, 80*

If this solemnity falls on a Sunday, it replaces the Sunday liturgy (as it will in 2001). Note that this day has a Vigil, which has its own readings.

Today is a nativity festival, also called Midsummer Day, Christmas's "alter ego." The wonderful story of the birth of John is detailed and wonderful reading, but this story is perhaps not all that well known. Perhaps the art here can be used to help tell the story. Other images of John are on pages 3, 12 and 14.

The daisy is associated with this solemnity: It means "day's eye," a synonym for the sun. Other appropriate images for Midsummer Day include the sun (pages 21 and 42) and summer fruits (pages 42, 47, 58 and 59).

Jesus identifies John the Baptist as Elijah, who is to return from heaven to announce the coming of the Messiah. The fiery chariot in this art is also a sign of the sun. Elijah's name in Greek, *Elias,* is like the Greek word for the sun, *'Elios.* A few writers of the early church thought that this was a splendid coincidence.

52

Thirteenth Sunday in Ordinary Time

green

June 27, 1993
June 30, 1996
June 27, 1999

2 Kings 4:8−11, 14−16
Psalm 89
Romans 6:3−4, 8−11
Matthew 10:37−42

For an illustration for the second reading, see page 62. Note the illustrations on this page and page 54 for Independence Day and other summertime events.

BAPTIZED INTO CHRIST'S DEATH

Ss. Peter and Paul

red

Tuesday, June 29, 1993
Saturday, June 29, 1996
Tuesday, June 29, 1999

Vigil	**Day**
Acts 3:1–10	*Acts 12:1–11*
Psalm 19:2–5	*Psalm 34*
Galatians 1:11–20	*2 Timothy 4:6–8, 17–18*
John 21:15–19	*Matthew 16:13–19*

If this solemnity falls on a Sunday, it replaces the Sunday liturgy (as it will in 1997). Note that it has a Vigil.

Peter and Paul are the "pillars of the church." Both came to be known for their preaching, for their founding care of Christian communities, for their martyrdom in Rome. The upside-down cross and the sword were, according to tradition, the instruments of execution of Peter and of Paul.

For other appropriate art for this day, see pages 38, 63 (St. Peter), and 14, 62 and 69 (St. Paul).

54

Fourteenth Sunday in Ordinary Time

green

July 4, 1993
July 7, 1996
July 4, 1999

Zechariah 9:9–10
   Psalm 145
Romans 8:9, 11–13
Matthew 11:25–30

For an illustration for the second reading, see page 62.

In 1993 and 1999 in the U.S.A., Independence Day may be in the forefront of most everyone's mind this Sunday, but the national holiday does not substitute for the Lord's Day in the liturgy of the church. The worship program might include holiday greetings (and a bit of Independence Day art) on the last page, but it probably would be inappropriate to include more than this in a worship aid this weekend.

Note the illustrations for Independence Day and other summertime events on this page and page 52. Other art for national holidays is on page 83.

55

Fifteenth Sunday in Ordinary Time

green

July 11, 1993
July 14, 1996
July 11, 1999

Isaiah 55:10–11
Psalm 65
Romans 8:18–23
Matthew 13:1–23

All three readings are illustrated here. For another illustration for the second reading, see page 62.

This is the first of three Sundays on which we hear several of the often familiar but sometimes surprising parables in Matthew's gospel. In keeping with the parable of the sower and the seed, other art on this page is appropriate for garden clubs and community gardens.

56

Sixteenth Sunday in Ordinary Time

green

July 18, 1993
July 21, 1996
July 18, 1999

Wisdom 12:13, 16–19
  Psalm 86
Romans 8:26–27
Matthew 13:24–43

For an illustration for the second reading, see page 62.

There are several parables in this Sunday's gospel: another parable about sowing seed, the parable of the mustard seed and the parable of hidden leaven; some of last Sunday's art is also appropriate for this Sunday.

57

Seventeenth Sunday in Ordinary Time

green

July 25, 1993
July 28, 1996
July 25, 1999

I Kings 3:5, 7–12
  Psalm 119:57, 72, 76–77, 127–130
Romans 8:28–30
Matthew 13:44–52

For an illustration for the second reading, see page 62.

58

Eighteenth Sunday in Ordinary Time

green

August 1, 1993
August 4, 1996
August 1, 1999

Isaiah 55:1–3
Psalm 145
Romans 8:35, 37–39
Matthew 14:13–21

All three readings are illustrated here. For another
illustration for the second reading, see page 62.

Note the illustrations of the miracle of loaves and fishes.

Transfiguration of the Lord

white

Friday, August 6, 1993
Tuesday, August 6, 1996
Friday, August 6, 1999

Daniel 7:9–10, 13–14
Psalm 97
2 Peter 1:16–19
Matthew 17:1–9

If this feast falls on a Sunday, it replaces the Sunday liturgy (as it does in 1995 and 2000).

For other appropriate art for this day, see page 25.

The feast comes 40 days before the feast of the Triumph of the Cross. At one time, these 40 days were a kind of "Lent" in preparation for autumn.

Jesus' transfiguration on Tabor is an epiphany, a revelation of who Jesus is and to what his followers are called. We are summoned up the mountain to enter into glory. The suffering and glory of flesh and blood is a powerful image that runs through the feasts of August and September.

This feast coincides with the tragic anniversary of the first use of nuclear weapons in war, in Hiroshima, Japan. In some parishes it is a day marked with fasting and prayer for peace.

The blessing of fruit was once customary on this day. The fruitfulness of August gardens is an image of the transfiguration of Jesus.

60

Nineteenth Sunday in Ordinary Time

green

August 8, 1993
August 11, 1996
August 8, 1999

1 Kings 19:9, 11–13
  Psalm 85
Romans 9:1–5
Matthew 14:22–33

For an illustration for the second reading, see page 62.

The bar of art on the left side of the page represents Psalm 85:10—"Love and fidelity will meet; justice and peace will kiss."

Note the images of Elijah; we "met" the prophet on Transfiguration Day. The fiery chariot that carried Elijah into heaven is depicted on page 51.

The coming Assumption holy day can receive attention this Sunday; you might feature the worship schedule prominently and avoid adding things that compete for attention so that the holy day material stands out. Some parishes send home prayers and ideas for other ways to observe the festival.

61

Assumption of Mary

white

Sunday, August 15, 1993
Thursday, August 15, 1996
Sunday, August 15, 1999

Vigil

1 Chronicles 15:3–4, 15, 16;
*   16:1–2*
Psalm 132
1 Corinthians 15:54–57
Luke 11:27–28

Day

Revelation 11:19; 12:1–6, 10
*   Psalm 45*
1 Corinthians 15:20–26
Luke 1:39–56

See page 4 for other art appropriate to this day.

This is the solemnity of the death, burial and resurrection of Mary—her passover. In ancient times in the churches of the West (and in many Eastern Rite churches today), the festival began with an all-night vigil in mourning for the death of Mary, which ended at dawn with a celebration of her resurrection.

In 1950, Pope Pius XII first defined the dogma of the Assumption. He did this partly as a response to the horrors of the Second World War, especially the concentration camps, and to the escalating threat of global nuclear war. Here in this solemnity is a sign of the dignity of the created world, the destiny of flesh and blood. Is it coincidence that August 15 is the anniversary of the day World War II ended?

Be sure the holy day worship schedule is displayed prominently in the bulletin so people can find it easily. Perhaps box the schedule, make it as large as possible and leave plenty of blank space around it. Include information about the solemnity as well as table prayers, songs and customs (for example, call attention to the Assumption Day blessing of produce in *Catholic Household Blessings and Prayers*) so that this day can be observed better at home as well as at worship.

Assumption Day is a celebration of the goodness of creation. The blessing of flowers, herbs and garden produce is traditional on this day (see chapter 28 of the *Book of Blessings*), especially in rural areas. In some coastal areas, the sea is blessed. All creation joins in thanksgiving as the first of God's creatures enters into glory.

Summer fruit and flowers are illustrated on pages 47, 48, 51, 54, 58, 59, 63, 64 and 79. On pages 55, 74 and 82 are other images of the summertime harvest. On pages 12, 15 and 57 are images of the sea.

62

Twentieth Sunday in Ordinary Time

green

August 18, 1996
(In 1993 and 1999, the Solemnity of the Assumption
   takes the place of this Sunday.)

Isaiah 56:1, 6–7
  Psalm 67
Romans 11:13–15, 29–32
Matthew 15:21–28

The illustration of Paul's Letter to the Romans (which is
proclaimed on summer Sundays in Year A) can be used
for worship programs whenever Romans is read.

***The images of musical instruments are useful in advertising
the parish music ministry.*** Note also the art for choir
practice on page 70. No doubt it's time to advertise
the parish's fall season of programs and ministries.
Other art for this purpose can be found on pages 70,
72 and 73.

63

Twenty-first Sunday in Ordinary Time

green

August 22, 1993
August 25, 1996
August 22, 1999

Isaiah 22:15, 19–23
   Psalm 138
Romans 11:33–36
Matthew 16:13–20

For an illustration for the second reading, see page 62.

64

Twenty-second Sunday in Ordinary Time

green

August 29, 1993
September 1, 1996
August 29, 1999

Jeremiah 20:7–9
  Psalm 63
Romans 12:1–2
Matthew 16:21–27

All three readings are illustrated here. For another illustration for the second reading, see page 62.

In 1996, this is Labor Day weekend. Appropriate art is on page 83. Art for "back to school" is on page 66.

Twenty-third Sunday in Ordinary Time

green

September 5, 1993
September 8, 1996
September 5, 1999

Ezekiel 33:7–9
  Psalm 95
Romans 13:8–10
Matthew 18:15–20

All three readings are illustrated here. For another illustration for the second reading, see page 62. Some of the art for this Sunday is useful in the bulletin as a "logo" for prayer groups.

In 1993 and 1999, this is Labor Day weekend. Appropriate art is on page 83.

66

Twenty-fourth Sunday in Ordinary Time

green

September 12, 1993
September 15, 1996
September 12, 1999

Sirach 27:30—28:7
  Psalm 103
Romans 14:7–9
Matthew 18:21–35

All three readings are illustrated here. For another illustration for the second reading, see page 62.

This Sunday we begin in Matthew's gospel a series of five Sundays on which we hear parables about God's reign.

Note the art useful for back-to-school activities. Note also the art appropriate to communal penance.

67

Triumph of the Cross

white

Tuesday, September 14, 1993
Saturday, September 14, 1996
Tuesday, September 14, 1999

Numbers 21:4—9
Psalm 78
Philippians 2:6—11
John 3:13—17

If this feast day falls on a Sunday, it replaces the Sunday liturgy (as it does in 1997).

The words "true" and "tree" are from the same source word; a truth is something deeply rooted. The tree of the cross, with its arms spread to the four corners, is a sign of that which is all-embracing, all-loving, all-truthful.

On this day in the year 335, the relic of the cross was first honored in Jerusalem. Since that occasion, in the Christian East the cross has been honored on this day with prayer and fasting, with flowers and glorious processions. This feast is like Good Friday. As autumn looms with its growing darkness, we raise the shining cross as our beacon and our treasure.

This feast day marks a turning point from summer into fall. It is a splendid day for liturgies for beginning religious education programs and the school year.

68

Autumn Ordinary Time Bulletin Cover

Tuesday, September 14, to Saturday, November 27, 1993
Saturday, September 14, to Saturday, November 30, 1996
Tuesday, September 14, to Saturday, November 27, 1999

For notes about Ordinary Time, see page 13.

In this book, Ordinary Time is divided into winter, summer and autumn. The feast of the Triumph of the Cross, September 14, and the feast of the archangels Michael, Gabriel and Raphael, September 29, have been customary days in parishes and religious communities for welcoming the fall and as a kickoff for church programs and ministries (for art, see pages 70, 72 and 73).

September is a kind of new year not just for schools but for many other organizations idled by summer.

In Year A, in the fall, our second readings at Sunday Mass are from Paul's Letter to the Philippians and then from Paul's First Letter to the Thessalonians. The first readings will be mainly from the prophets Isaiah, Ezekiel and Malachi. We conclude our yearlong reading from the gospel according to Matthew.

AUTUMN

69

Twenty-fifth Sunday in Ordinary Time

green

September 19, 1993
September 22, 1996
September 19, 1999

Isaiah 55:6–9
   Psalm 145
Philippians 1:20–24, 27
Matthew 20:1–16

All three readings are illustrated here.

On the Twenty-fifth through Twenty-eighth Sundays in Ordinary Time of Year A, the second readings are from the Letter of Paul to the Philippians. The "generic" art in the lower left corner of this page can be used to illustrate the letter on all the Sundays it's read.

The vineyard and harvest images of the Sunday readings are appropriate for the autumn season. On the next three Sundays, we will hear parables about the reign of heaven that use the image of a vineyard.

PHILIPPI

70

Twenty-sixth Sunday in Ordinary Time

green

September 26, 1993
September 29, 1996
September 26, 1999

Ezekiel 18:25–28
   Psalm 125
Philippians 2:1–11
Matthew 21:28–32

For an illustration for the second reading, see page 69.

*Several pieces of art on the next few pages are useful
year-round for the regular features of the parish bulletin.*
On this page is bulletin art for ushers, choirs, servers, eucharistic ministers and lectors. This art can be
used in the bulletin as the regular "logo" for items of
interest to these ministers.

ALTAR SERVERS

EUCHARISTIC MINISTERS

MINISTERS OF HOSPITALITY - USHERS

CHOIR

LECTORS

71

Twenty-seventh Sunday in Ordinary Time

green

October 3, 1993
October 6, 1996
October 3, 1999

Isaiah 5:1–7
  Psalm 80
Philippians 4:6–9
Matthew 21:33–43

All three readings are illustrated here. For another illustration for the second reading, see page 69.

72

Twenty-eighth Sunday in Ordinary Time

green

October 10, 1993
October 13, 1996
October 10, 1999

Isaiah 25:6–10
   Psalm 23
Philippians 4:12–14, 19–20
Matthew 22:1–14

For an illustration for the second reading, see page 69.

On this page is art that is useful year-round in the bulletin for the worship schedule, wedding banns and death notices. This art can be used in the bulletin as the regular "logo" for these items. Also here is art for advertising a potluck supper and for any festive gathering, such as a wedding.

DEATH NOTICES

MASS SCHEDULE

WEDDING BANNS

73

Twenty-ninth Sunday in Ordinary Time

green

October 17, 1993
October 20, 1996
October 17, 1999

Isaiah 45:1, 4–6
   Psalm 96
1 Thessalonians 1:1–5
Matthew 22:15–21

All three readings are illustrated here.

On the Twenty-ninth through Thirty-third Sundays in Ordinary Time of Year A, the second readings are from the First Letter of Paul to the Thessalonians. The art in the lower left corner of this page can be used to illustrate the letter.

Halloween is coming! The parish and school schedule for worship and other activities for the coming festival of Halloween, All Saints and All Souls can be advertised in the bulletin.

On this page is art that is useful year-round in the bulletin for the catechumenate. This art can be used in the bulletin as the regular "logo" for items of interest to these people.

RC IA

THESSALONIKA

Thirtieth Sunday in Ordinary Time

green

October 24, 1993
October 27, 1996
October 24, 1999

Exodus 22:20−26
Psalm 18
1 Thessalonians 1:5−10
Matthew 22:34−40

For an illustration for the second reading, see page 73.

Note the art for autumn and Halloween. Halloween is All Saints' Eve. The customs of Halloween are customs for November 1 and 2 as well. School personnel and those who prepare worship folders and parish bulletins can communicate this connection: Use some of the images ordinarily associated with Halloween, such as trick-or-treat, on the material you prepare for All Saints and All Souls. Use images associated with All Saints and All Souls, such as palm branches and gravestones, on the material you prepare for Halloween. See pages 76 and 77, and the other November pages, for art for these days.

Thirty-first Sunday in Ordinary Time

green

October 31, 1993
November 3, 1996
October 31, 1999

Malachi 1:14 — 2:2, 8 – 10
   Psalm 131
1 Thessalonians 2:7 – 9, 13
Matthew 23:1 – 12

All three readings are illustrated here. For another illustration for the second reading, see page 73. For an image of trick-or-treat, see page 74. Other art for Halloween can be gleaned from the next few pages.

In Year A, we have been reading through Matthew's gospel on the Sundays of Ordinary Time. Now, in late October and throughout November, we come to the final chapters before the account of the passion and death of Jesus. These chapters have an emphasis on the end of time, the glorious coming of Christ, the last judgment.

The eschatological accent of the gospel passages is supported by the strong end-of-the-world imagery of the First Letter of Paul to the Thessalonians, from which is drawn the second readings for these Sundays.

The feast days and the Sundays of November, while not a season like Advent or Christmastime, do hang together thematically. The liturgy this month is rich with the language of the harvest, of death, of eternity. We begin with All Saints' Day and the commemoration of All Souls, and we conclude with the solemnity of Christ the King, and, in the United States, with the national day of Thanksgiving.

When selecting images for a particular feast or Lord's Day in November, search through all the art for this month. Look through the art for Advent and for Eastertime as well.

Cornucopias and images of the harvest are just as at home on All Saints' Day as on Thanksgiving Day. Images of the last judgment, of the paschal lamb and of jack o'lanterns are as appropriate for all the Sundays of November as they are for All Souls.

76

All Saints

white

Monday, November 1, 1993
Friday, November 1, 1996
Monday, November 1, 1999

Revelation 7:2–4, 9–14
  Psalm 24
1 John 3:1–3
Matthew 5:1–12

All Saints is a great harvest homecoming festival of the church. As the preface to the eucharistic prayer for All Saints reminds us, on this day God's children are gathered into the holy city, Jerusalem, to begin the marriage supper of the Lamb.

Advertise All Saints and All Souls. In addition to the worship schedule for these days, perhaps there can be a few pastoral words of encouragement for the keeping of these days at home as well as in the parish. In the bulletin, devote as much attention as possible to these days. The bulletin can make it appear, in spirit at least, that parish programs and business-as-usual take a back seat to the festival.

LTP publishes a bulletin insert for Halloween, All Saints and All Souls. It's called *The Days of the Dead,* and it offers a refreshing, Christian perspective on the popular customs of these holy days.

Spooky images can be Christian symbols, strange as that may at first seem. Nocturnal animals such as owls and bats and the angel of death (sometimes represented as a skull, often carved into a pumpkin) are *memento mori,* reminders of death.

On All Saints and All Souls, we surround ourselves with these emblems and then announce with confidence, "Where, O death, is your sting? Where, O grave, is your victory? But thanks be to God, who gives us the victory through our Lord Jesus Christ!" (1 Corinthians 15:55, 57).

For your information, the five saints depicted in the art near the center top are St. Peter, St. Catherine of Alexandria, St. Francis of Assisi, St. Mary of Egypt and St. Benedict of Nursia.

77

All Souls

black, violet or white

Tuesday, November 2, 1993
Saturday, November 2, 1996
Tuesday, November 2, 1999

Readings for All Souls can draw from any of the readings for the Masses for the Dead; particularly appropriate for this day are:

Daniel 12:1–3
   Psalm 122 (November's "seasonal psalm")
Revelation 21:1–5, 6–7
Luke 12:35–40

Does this day receive the attention and dignity it deserves in the parish? If it falls on a weekday, extra efforts will be needed to encourage observance of the day and attendance at worship. The parish calendar can be kept free so the day is not business-as-usual for parish or school.

If it falls on a Saturday, has the calendar been blocked out so that weddings won't be scheduled for this day?

***Call attention to the appropriate prayers in* Catholic Household Blessings and Prayers.** All Saints and All Souls are good times to make this book available to the parish and to encourage its use.

See the other notes about November on page 75.

78

Thirty-second Sunday in Ordinary Time

green

November 7, 1993

November 10, 1996

November 7, 1999

Wisdom 6:12−16

  Psalm 63

1 Thessalonians 4:13−18

Matthew 25:1−13

All three readings are illustrated here. For another illustration for the second reading, see page 73.

See the notes about November on page 75.

Dedication of the Lateran Basilica

white

Tuesday, November 9, 1993
Saturday, November 9, 1996
Tuesday, November 9, 1999

Any readings from the common for the dedication of a church may be chosen.

This is the dedication anniversary of the cathedral of Rome, the "mother church" of Roman Catholics. The feast replaces the Sunday liturgy if it falls on a Lord's Day, as it will in 1997. The feast reflects a particularly rich image that comes to the fore in November—the coming down from heaven of Jerusalem, God's holy city, as bright as a bride.

This feast brings to mind the question: How does the parish celebrate the anniversary of its dedication? How does it celebrate its titular day (often also its patronal day)? These two occasions are "solemnities," the highest feast within the parish boundaries. How about the anniversary of the dedication of the cathedral and the patronal day of the diocese?

And how do you get the word out about these parish-wide or diocesan feast days? These are premier occasions to provide the parish with information about its history and a vision of where the parish is heading. The days need special liturgy, yes. But they need more. The patronal or dedication day may be a time for a parish picnic, an evening of recollection or even the annual parish mission.

Use the bulletin and other handouts to advertise at least a month or more in advance so parishioners can mark calendars and plan to attend. Search the index of this book for appropriate art.

URBS BEATA

JERUSALEM

ST. JOHN LATERAN

80

Thirty-third Sunday in Ordinary Time

green

November 14, 1993
November 17, 1996
November 14, 1999

Proverbs 31:10–13, 19–20, 30–31
  Psalm 128
1 Thessalonians 5:1–6
Matthew 25:14–30

All three readings are illustrated here. For another illustration for the second reading, see page 73.

See the notes about November on page 75.

Christic the King

white

Last Sunday in Ordinary Time

November 21, 1993
November 24, 1996
November 21, 1999

Ezekiel 34:11–12, 15–17
    Psalm 23
1 Corinthians 15:20–26, 28
Matthew 25:31–46

See the notes about November on page 75.

In some years, this solemnity falls after Thanksgiving (in the U.S.A.). In 1993, 1996 and 1999, it falls before Thanksgiving. Christ the King is always the Sunday before Advent begins.

Christ the King and the earlier Sundays of November can be used as a preparation for the coming season. Is the word out about parish plans for Advent and Christmastime? How much effort is being put into education about the nature of Advent and the possible ways of observing the season? The bulletin this week can be put to the service of reminding us about Advent. This Sunday is a good time to make materials (and explanations) available for making Advent wreaths.

TURKEY SALE

82

Thanksgiving Day

white

**In Canada,
the second Monday in October:**

October 11, 1993

October 14, 1996

October 11, 1999

**In the U.S.A.,
the fourth Thursday in November:**

November 25, 1993

November 28, 1996

November 25, 1999

Readings may be chosen from the weekday; from the Masses for various public needs, "after the harvest" or "in thanksgiving"; or from the votive Mass for Thanksgiving Day.

In the bulletin, call attention to the appropriate prayers for this day in *Catholic Household Blessings and Prayers.* LTP publishes a bulletin insert for Thanksgiving, called *Come, Ye Thankful People, Come,* which is inexpensive and sold in packages of 100. Included is a meal prayer, a psalm and a reflection on the significance of this beloved holiday.

83

National Days

Martin Luther King, Jr., Birthday
January 15,
observed on the third Monday in January

Lincoln's Birthday
February 12

Presidents' Day
third Monday in February

Washington's Birthday
February 22

Victoria Day
Monday closest to May 24

Memorial Day
last Monday in May

Canada Day
July 1

Independence Day
July 4

Labor Day
first Monday in September

Columbus Day
October 12,
observed on the Second Monday in October

Election Day
first Tuesday after the first Monday in November
  in the U.S.A.

Veteran's Day
November 11

Remembrance Day
November 11

Search the index for other art for national holidays;
for example, fireworks (pages 52 and 54) or cherries
(page 47).

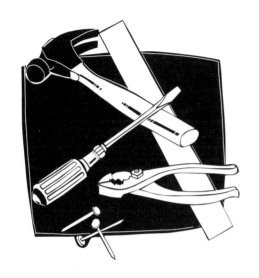

IN MEMORIAM

84

Index

Abraham, 48
Abraham and Sarah, 25
Adam and Eve, 24
Advent, 1–6
Advent wreath, 5
Agony in the garden, 29
All Saints' Day, 76
All Souls' Day, 77
Alleluia, 33, 37
Almsgiving, 18, 20, 23, 24
Alpha and Omega, 81
Angel, 61
  appearing to Joseph, 9
  at the tomb, 33
  guarding the gates of Eden, 58
  with sickle, 79
  with scroll, 4, 8
  with trumpet, 7, 8, 75
Angel of death, 31
Angels
  at the Ascension, 41
  on Jacob's ladder, 63
  singing "glad new year," 10
  with cross, 67
Animals, 53
Anna, St., 17
Anointing, 27
Apostles, 15, 36, 42, 43
Apple blossoms, 41
Apples and pears, 63
Apricots, 47
"Are you he who is to come?" 5
Ascension, 34, 41
Ash Wednesday, 23
Assumption of Mary, 61
Autumn flowers, 79
Autumn leaves, 73, 76, 80, 81
Baking, 56
Banquet, 58, 72
Baptism, 33, 45, 52, 73
Baptism of the Lord, 12
"Baptized into Christ's death," 52
Basin and towel, 31
Bean vines, 55
"Behold the Lamb of God," 14
Birds, 2, 18, 21, 45, 50, 67
  in nest, 40, 50
Birth of John the Baptist, 51
Blood of the Lamb, 31
"Blow the trumpet in Zion," 23
Boat, 4, 15, 57, 58
Body and Blood of Christ, 46
Book, 21
Book of the dead, 77
Books, 69
Bread and cup, 18, 31, 42, 46
Bridesmaids, wise and foolish, 78
Broom, 80
Burning bush, 26
Butterfly, 37
Buying a turkey, 81
Cain and Abel, 71

Candle(s), 66
  and flowers and snow, 17
  children holding, 80
  Easter, 33, 73
  in lamp, 65
  in window, 14
  with book, 21
  with incense, 28
Candlemas, 17
Carnival, 19
Caroling, 9
Cecilia, St., 78
Cemetery, 77
Charity, 18, 20, 23
Cherries, 47, 83
Children, 80
"Children of the light," 27, 80
Choir, 70
Christmas, 7–10
City, 20
Clouds, 41, 48
"Come, all you who are thirsty," 58
Comedy and tragedy, 19
Comet, 11
Corinthians, first letter of Paul
  to the, 14
Corn, 55, 74, 81, 82
Cornucopia, 82
Crocus, 24
Cross, 32, 50, 67, 74
Crowning with thorns, 32
Crowns, 11
Crucifixion, 32, 49, 67
Cyrus the King, 73
Daisies, 51
Daughter of Zion, 54
David the King, 27, 62
Deacons, 39
Death notices, 72
Death's head, 77
Decorating with evergreens, 6
Dedication of Lateran Basilica, 79
Deer, 39
Demon(s), 24, 25, 40, 64
Desert in bloom, 5
Disciples in the upper room, 36, 42
Dog, 62, 63
Dormition of Mary, 61
Dough, 56
Doughnuts, 19
Dove, 12, 43, 45
Dove and wolf, 47
Doves, 17
Eagle, 49
Earth, 41
Easter, 33–43
Easter bunny, 36, 37
Easter candle, 33, 73
Easter eggs, 36, 37
Easter fire, 33
Easter sequence, 35
Easter Vigil, 33

Elijah
  at the transfiguration, 25, 59
  fed by raven, 60
  in cave, 60
  in fiery chariot, 51
Elisha, 52
Elizabeth, St., 51
Emmaus, 36, 37
Empty tomb, 36
Epiphany, 11, 12
Eucharist, 36, 46
Eucharistic ministers, 70
Evangelists, **67**
Exodus, 33, 54
Family scene, 9, 39, 82
"Farmer longing for the harvest," 5
Fasting, 23, 26
Father Time (St. Sylvester), 10
Feeding the hungry, 18
Fiery chariot, 51
Fiery furnace, 45
Fire, 33, 60
Fireworks, 52, 54
Fish, 12, 15
  grilled, 38, 58
  in net, 15, 57
Fishermen, 15, 57
Flight into Egypt, 9
Flowers: see "spring," "summer,"
  "autumn"
Flowerpot, 24
Food, 72
Foot washing, 31, 75
Forgiveness, 40, 66
Fountain, 35, 39, 40
Frog, 36
Fruit, 59
Gabriel, Archangel, 4
"Gate of the sheepfold," 38
"Get behind me, Satan," 64
"Give Caesar what is Caesar's," 73
Gold, frankincense, myrrh, 11
Good Friday, 32
Good Shepherd, 38
Gourds, 74
Grapes, 16, 69
Graves, 28, 75, 77
"Greatest will serve the least," 75
Grim reaper, 75
Hagia Sophia, 1
Halloween, 74, 76
Harvest, 49, 81, 82
Heart with cross, 40, 65
Hearts, 19
"Herald's voice in the desert," 3
Holy Family, 8, 9, 10
Holy Spirit, 12, 34, 42, 43, 45, 56
Holy Thursday, 31
Hot cross buns, 35
"House built on rock," 47
Husband and wife, 80
Immaculate Conception, 4

"In my father's house," 39
Incense, 9, 28, 51, 65, 71
Independence Day, 52, 54, 83
Iris, 20
Jack o'lanterns, 76
Jacob's ladder, 63
Jeremiah, 2, 64
Jerusalem, 11, 39, 79
Jesse tree, 3
Jester, 19
Jesus
  at his baptism, 12
  at his birth, 7, 8, 9
  at his circumcision, 10
  at his epiphany, 11, 12
  at his presentation, 17
  at his transfiguration, 25, 59
  at the Last Supper, 29, 31
  betrayed by Judas, 29
  calling Matthew, 48
  crucified, 32, 49, 67
  entering Jerusalem, 29
  gardener, 35, 81
  good shepherd, 38
  healing the man born blind, 27
  in a boat, 58
  in Gethsemane, 29
  King and judge, 2, 41, 66, 68, 81
  lamb of God, 14
  lord of the harvest, 81
  multiplying loaves and fishes,
    44, 58
  new Adam, 50
  on the road to Emmaus, 37
  raising Lazarus, 28
  risen from the dead, 30, 34,
    35, 36
  suffering servant, 32
  teacher, 2, 5, 13, 15, 16, 73
  tempted by Satan, 24
  walking on water, 44, 60
  washing feet, 31
  whose yoke is easy, 54
  with Canaanite woman, 62
  with Peter, 63, 64
  with the Samaritan woman, 26
  with Thomas, 36
  with the wild beasts, 24
John the Baptist, 3, 12, 14
  birth of, 51
Jonah in the fish, 38
Jordan River, 12
Joseph, St., 6, 8, 9, 10
Judas Iscariot, 29
Judge, 56
"Keep watch," 2, 78, 80
Key of David, 63
King, Martin Luther, Jr., 83
Kneading dough, 56
Labor Day, 83
Laetare, 27
Lamb of God, 36, 37, 38

Lamp, 16
   oil, 78
   on bushel basket, 18
Last Judgment, 2, 41, 66, 68, 75, 78, 81
Last Supper, 29, 31
Lazarus, 28
Lectors, 70
Lent, 22–29
Liberty bell, 83
Lilies, 4, 36
"Little child will lead them," 3
Loaves and fishes, 44, 58
"Love of God poured out in our hearts," 26
Love one another, 40
Love your neighbor, 20, 65, 74
Lucy, St., 5
Magi, 11
Man born blind, 27
Man with two sons, 70
Manna, 46
Martin Luther King, Jr., 83
Martin of Tours, St., 78
Mary, 4, 6, 7, 8, 9, 10, 11, 17, 42, 43, 61
Mary and Joseph, 7, 8, 9, 10
Mary Magdalene at the tomb, 35
Mass schedule, 72
"Master of the house," 66
Matthew, St., 48
Matthias, St., 42
Memorial Day, 83
Mistletoe, 6
Money, 48
Moon, 69
   and sun, 49
   and 12 stars, 4
Mors et vita duello, 35
Moses
   and the ten commandments, 47
   at transfiguration of Jesus, 25, 59
   and the people, 47
   on the mountain, 49
   water from the rock, 26
Mother and child, 21, 52, 75
Musical instruments, 62
"My Father's house," 39
"My yoke is easy," 54
National holidays, 83
Nets, 15, 57
New Year's Day, 10
Nicholas of Myra, St., 3
Noah's ark, 30
November, 75–82
O Antiphons, 6
Oak leaves, 73, 76, 80, 81
Oil (chrism), 27
Oil lamp, 78
Olive branch, 29
Orphans and widows, 74
Our Lady of Guadalupe, 5

Owl, 76, 77
Palms, 29, 53, 76
Palm Sunday, 29
Paradise, 24, 50, 58
Paschal candle, 33, 73
Paschal lamb, 36, 37, 38
Paschal Triduum, 30–33, 35
Passion Sunday, 29
Passion symbols, 32
Passover, 30, 31, 33, 54
Paul of Tarsus, St., 14, 53, 62, 69
"Peace to you," 36
Peace and justice, 2, 3, 56, 60
Peaches, 59
Peacock, 39, 40
Pearls, 57
Pears and apples, 63
Pelican, 39
Pentecost, 42, 43
Pentecost novena, 42
Pentecost sequence, 43
Peonies, 43
People, 16, 48, 56
People murmuring, 50
Peter at the tomb, 35
Peter, St., 38, 53, 63, 64
Peter and Paul, Ss., 53
Pheasants, 77
Philip, St., 40
Philippians, letter of Paul to, 69
Phoenix, 39
Piggy bank, 24
Pine, 3
Poinsettia, 9
Pomegranates, 79
Poppies, 42,
Prayer, 9, 56, 65, 70, 71
"Prepare the way of the Lord," 3
Presentation in the temple, 17
Presidents' Day, 83
Procession, 29, 46, 76
Prophets, 1, 35
Pumpkins, 76, 82
Pussy willows, 23
Rabbit, 36, 37, 57
Rain, 48
Rain and snow, 55
Rainbow, 37
Raising of Lazarus, 28
Rake, 80
Ram's horn (shofar), 23
Raven, 28, 60, 75
RCIA, 73
Readers (lectors), 70
Reconciliation, 66
Rejoice, 27
"Rejoice, daughter of Zion," 54
"Remember, people, you are dust," 22
Remembering the dead, 77
Romans, letter of Paul to, 62
Rome, 53

Rooster, 32
Roses, 6, 9, 27
Rosette (design from Moissac), 60
Sacrifice, 62
Saints, 38, 76
Samaritan woman, 26
Samuel, 27
Sandals, 52
School bus, 66
Scorpion, 24, 25
Scrutiny rites, 26, 27, 28
Seedlings, 55
Sermon on the mount, 13, 16
Servers, 70
Shamrocks, 28
"Share bread with the hungry," 18
Sheep, 8, 38
Shepherds, 8, 10
Sickle, 49
Simeon, St., 17
Singers, 9, 62
Skull, 28, 75, 77
Snake, 25, 32, 54
Snow, 10
Snow and rain, 55
Solomon the King, 57
Sorrow, 55
Soup, 23, 26
Soup kitchen, 82
Sower and seed, 44, 55
Sparrows, 50
Spear, 32
Sponge, 32
Spring flowers, 20, 24, 25, 41, 42, 43, 54
Squashes, 82
Star, 11
Star of the sea, 4
Stars, 52
Stars and stripes, 83
Strawberries, 42, 47
Summer camp, 63, 64
Summer flowers, 42, 43, 48, 51, 54
Summer fruit, 47, 58, 59, 63, 64
Sun, 21, 42
   and moon, 49
   and tents, 59
Sunflower, 61
Sun of justice, 6
Swords into ploughshares, 2
Sylvester, St., 10
Tangerines, 3
Taxes, 48
Teacher, 16
Temple, 20, 62
Ten Commandments, 26, 47
"Tenants kill vineyard owner's son," 71
Thanksgiving dinner, 82
Thessalonians, first letter of Paul to the, 73
Thirst, 52

"Thirsting for God," 64
Thomas, St., 36
Three youths in fiery furnace, 45
Tombstone, 75
Tongues of fire, 43
Tools, 83
Tower, 71
Transfiguration, 25, 59
"Treasure buried in a field," 57
Tree, 19, 50
Tree of knowledge, 50
Trick or treat, 74
Trinity, 45
Triumph of the Cross, 67
Ushers, 70
Valentines, 19
Veterans Day, 83
Vine, 46, 69
Vineyard, 71
"Virgin shall be with child," 6
"Wake from your sleep," 2
Walnuts, 3
Watchman, 65
Water, 12, 15, 45, 57
"Water from the rock," 26
Watermelon, 58
Wedding banns, 72
Wheat, 5, 15, 46, 49, 82
Wheat and grapes, 46
"Where two or three are gathered in my name," 65
Wind, 43, 60
Winter clothing, 20
Winter scene, 14, 18
Wisdom, 1
Wise and foolish bridesmaids, 78
Wolf and dove, 47
Woman at the well, 26
Wreath
   Advent, 5
   of flowers, 59
   of oak leaves, 76
   memorial, 83
Yoke, 54
Zachary, St. (Zechariah, John's father), 51